RESOURCE
BOOKS FOR
TEACHERS

series editor
ALAN MALEY

CW00542858

DRAMA WITH CHILDREN

Sarah Phillips

OXFORD

UNIVERSITY PRESS

Oxford University Press
Great Clarendon Street, Oxford OX2 6DP

Oxford New York
Athens Auckland Bangkok Bogotá
Buenos Aires Calcutta Cape Town Chennai
Dar es Salaam Delhi Florence Hong Kong
Istanbul Karachi Kuala Lumpur Madrid
Melbourne Mexico City Mumbai Nairobi
Paris São Paulo Singapore Taipei Tokyo
Toronto Warsaw

and associated companies in
Berlin Ibadan

Oxford and *Oxford English*
are trade marks of Oxford University Press

ISBN 0 19 437220 0

Photocopying

Illustrations by Margaret Welbank
Cover illustration by Val Saunders

Typeset by Oxford University Press

Printed in Hong Kong

Acknowledgements

I would like to thank the many people have played a part in this book. These include the teachers, colleagues, and friends who have inspired and encouraged me, in particular Cova Ródriguez, Janet Torres, Denise O'Brian, M. Carmen Liñares, and Cristina Castro, who have all read and commented on the manuscript. Also, Belinda Fenn and Julia Sallabank at Oxford University Press, who have used their professional expertise to help make a coherent book from a ragged manuscript, and anonymous readers whose opinions have contributed to the shape and direction of the book. Finally of course, Angeles and Jan, who have sung, danced, mimed, and acted their way throughout the writing of it. I would like to thank all of you.

The publishers and author would like to thank the following for their kind permission to reproduce extracts from works published by them.

IQ Music for 'Who stole the cookie from the cookie jar' by Zelma Sanders.

A & C Black (Publishers) Limited for their arrangement of 'The Princess' from *Okki-tokki-unga*©, Action songs for children chosen by Beatrice Harrop, Linda Friend, and David Gadsby. A & C Black, London.

Every effort has been made to trace the owners of copyright material in this book, but we should be pleased to hear from any copyright holder whom we have been unable to contact. We apologise for any apparent negligence. If notified, the publisher will be pleased to rectify any errors or omissions at the earliest opportunity.

Contents

The author and series editor

Sarah Phillips trained as an English Language teacher at the Bell School, Norwich, and took her MA in ELT at Edinburgh University. She has held various teaching posts in Europe and has taught on primary teacher training courses with the Norwich Institute of Language Education. She has worked with the Regional Government of Galicia to prepare training courses and materials for teachers of English. She was part of a team that produced a video of children's songs and games with LINGUA support. At the moment she is working on a textbook for children and teaching at the Instituto de Idiomas at the University of Santiago de Compostela. She is the author of *Young Learners*.

Alan Maley worked for The British Council from 1962 to 1988, serving as English Language Officer in Yugoslavia, Ghana, Italy, France, and China, and as Regional Representative for The British Council in South India (Madras). From 1988 to 1993 he was Director-General of the Bell Educational Trust, Cambridge. From 1993 to 1998 he was Senior Fellow in the Department of English Language and Literature of the National University of Singapore. He is currently a freelance consultant and Director of the graduate English programme at Assumption University, Bangkok. He wrote *Quartet* (with Françoise Grellet and Wim Welsing, OUP 1982), and *Literature*, in this series (with Alan Duff, OUP 1990). He has also written *Beyond Words*, *Sounds Interesting*, *Sounds Intriguing*, *Words*, *Variations on a Theme*, and *Drama Techniques in Language Learning* (all with Alan Duff), *The Mind's Eye* (with Françoise Grellet and Alan Duff), and *Learning to Listen* and *Poem into Poem* (with Sandra Moulding). He is also Series Editor for the New Perspectives and Oxford Supplementary Skills series.

Foreword

Children, perhaps more than any other category of learners, delight in make-believe. They are immediately at home in imaginary worlds, where they can act out a role, engage in 'pretend' activities, dress up, and for a short while become another person.

Language teachers at this level commonly have to face two difficulties however. On the one hand, they need to channel the naturally exuberant imaginative energy of the children into activity which is not merely enjoyable but which also has a language pay-off. On the other, they need to develop a repertoire of concrete activities which appeal to the children: failure to do so will result in chaos or boredom.

In this new book, Sarah Phillips comprehensively addresses these two needs. She offers carefully structured activities with clearly articulated educational and language teaching aims. And the book brings together a collection of ideas, texts, and activities which the busy teacher of young children can draw upon to suit the needs of her own class. It begins with dramatization activities, such as mime, and goes on to the use of songs, rhymes, and chants, the making and use of puppets, and the use of playscripts. It culminates with slightly more advanced role play and simulation activities.

As the demand for English for younger learners continues to grow, so too does the demand for reliable and stimulating teaching materials. This collection represents a significant addition to the resources available to teachers at this level, and is a fitting extension of the work available in Sarah Phillips' earlier book in this series, *Young Learners*, which has already proved such a well-tried favourite.

Alan Maley

Introduction

Who is this book for?

Children

Nearly all the activities in this book have been used in the classroom with children between the ages of five and twelve at different levels. Of course, other factors affect the suitability of the individual activities for different children: the amount of drama they have done before, the kind of teaching environment they are used to, their gender, the atmosphere in the classroom, and cultural attitudes towards physical expression. The teacher is the best person to decide how these factors affect his or her class. Therefore, the recommended ages and levels in each activity are given for guidance only.

Teachers

This book is for both inexperienced and experienced primary-level language teachers who are interested in introducing, or developing, drama as an extra dimension in their teaching. It provides practical introductory activities for teachers who have never used drama in their classrooms before. There are also more ambitious activities, like plays and improvisations, for those who feel more confident about using drama as an integral part of their lessons, or who want to prepare a performance such as an end-of-term show. The aim is to provide a practical introduction to dramatizing in the classroom and to provide a starting-point from which teachers can develop ideas of their own.

Dramatizing not drama

The word drama may produce the image of an end-of-term play, staged by nervous children, organized by overwrought teachers, and watched by fond parents. I want to replace this image with a much less dramatic one. Drama is not only about the product (the performance) but part of the process of language learning. It allows children to own the simple and mechanical language they use by involving their personalities. It gives those children who are shy when speaking a foreign language another character to 'hide behind'. 'Dramatizing' is perhaps a better word for this than drama: dramatizing is much simpler than that nerve-racking end-of-term play. Dramatizing means that the children become actively involved in a text. This personalization makes language more meaningful and memorable than drilling or mechanical repetition can.

Why use drama activities?

Using drama and drama activities has clear advantages for language learning. It encourages children to speak and gives them the chance to communicate, even with limited language, using non-verbal communication, such as body movements and facial expressions. There are also a number of other factors which make drama a very powerful tool in the language classroom. Try thinking about the ways in which reading a dialogue aloud from a textbook is different from acting out that same dialogue. You will find that the list is a long one. This is because drama involves children at many levels, through their bodies, minds, emotions, language, and social interaction. Some of the areas where I feel drama is very useful to language learners and teachers are outlined below.

Motivation

Dramatizing a text is very motivating and it's fun. In addition, the same activity can be done at different levels at the same time, which means that all the children can do it successfully. The end product, the performance, is clear and so children feel safe, and have a goal to work towards (even though this may not coincide with their teacher's aims). Children are motivated if they know that one or two groups will be asked to show what they have done, or if they are being videoed or putting on a public performance.

Familiar activities

Dramatizing is part of children's lives from an early age: children act out scenes and stories from the age of about three or four. They play at being adults in situations, like shopping and visiting the doctor, which are part of their lives. Many of these day-to-day situations are predictable. Children try out different roles in make-believe play. They rehearse the language and the 'script' of the situation and experience the emotions involved, knowing that they can switch back to reality whenever they want to.

Such pretend play prepares children for the real-life situations they will meet later on: it is a rehearsal of the real thing. Make-believe encourages their creativity and develops their imagination, and at the same time gives them the opportunity to use language that is outside their daily needs. Language teachers can use this natural desire to act out situations. You can ask them to be Little Red Riding Hood, Aladdin's Magic Carpet, or a bank robber and then use all the language that grows out of that personality or role.

Confidence

By taking on a role, children can escape from their everyday identity and lose their inhibitions. This is useful with children who are shy about speaking English, or don't like joining in group activities. If you give them a special role it encourages them to be that character and abandon their shyness or embarrassment. This is especially true when you use puppets and masks. The teacher can use roles to encourage children who would otherwise hold back, and control children who dominate the weaker ones.

Group dynamics

Children often work in groups or pairs when dramatizing. This group work may be very structured, where children reproduce a model, or it may mean children taking responsibility for their own work. Children have to make decisions as a group, listen to each other, and value each other's suggestions. They have to co-operate to achieve their aims, find ways of settling their differences, and use the strengths of each member of the group.

Different learning styles

Dramatizing appeals to all kinds of learners. We receive and process information in different ways, the main ones are through sight, hearing, and our physical bodies. One of these channels tends to be dominant in each of us. If we receive new information through this channel, it is easier for us to understand and use; if it is presented through a weaker channel, we tend to find the ideas more difficult. When children dramatize they use all the channels, and each child will draw on the one that suits them best. This means they will all be actively involved in the activity and the language will 'enter' through the channel most appropriate for them.

Language personalization

Dramatizing allows children to add an emotion or personality to a text that they have read or listened to. Take any word, sentence, or short dialogue (two to four lines) and ask the children to practise saying it 'in character'. It is surprising how the meaning of something as simple as 'What's your name?' can be changed according to how and where you say it. Think about how a policeman asks a robber and how Father Christmas asks a hopeful child this same question. By interpreting the words, the children make them their own. This also makes language memorable.

Language in context

In the classroom, we often expose children to small bits of language such as individual words, rather than whole phrases or 'chunks'. When speaking, children are not often asked to combine the different structures they are learning. Drama is an ideal way to encourage children to guess the meaning of unknown language in a context which often makes meaning clear. Similarly, children will need to use a mixture of language structures and functions if they are to communicate successfully.

Cross-curricular content

When using drama your aims can be more than linguistic. You can use topics from other subjects: the children can act out scenes from history, or the life cycle of a frog. You can work on ideas and issues that run through the curriculum, such as sexism, respect for the environment, and road safety. Important messages can be conveyed and explored through sketches and role play. Drama can also be used to introduce the culture of the new language, through stories and customs, and with a context for working on different kinds of behaviour.

The pace of a lesson

Drama can add a change of pace or mood to the classroom. Dramatizing is learner-centred so that you can use it to contrast with the more teacher-centred parts of your lesson. It is active and so you can use it to make a class more lively after quieter or individual work.

Practical advice on using dramatization in the classroom

Choose the right activity

When you plan a drama activity you need to know your aim. There are activities for accuracy and fluency work, and others that practise language skills. Your aim may be to revise and practise language from previous lessons, or it may be to change the pace of the lesson. Look at the focus column of the contents page at the beginning of the book.

The children's age affects the kind of activity you plan. Younger children find it more difficult to work in groups and so whole-class activities, or very guided activities, are better for them. Older children may work better in smaller groups, though this depends on the style of teaching they are used to. They may take more initiative, contributing their own ideas about characters and situations, and if they have been attending English classes for some time, will perhaps only need the teacher to help with language. The more dramatization the children do, and the more they reflect on what they have done, the better they will become at it.

Start small

Not all children are good at acting, especially if drama is not part of their first language curriculum. Introduce drama into your classroom in small steps. Start with easy, guided activities, such as 1.1 'Mime a monster', and move on to less controlled activities, such as the plays, as the children gain confidence. You may be surprised that you need to teach them simple things like stretching out their arms, taking big and small steps, and using their faces and whole bodies to show emotion. 'Total Physical Response' activities are an excellent way into dramatization: the children respond to language with their bodies, a first step to miming and acting. Children often don't realize that they can say things in different ways: simply asking them to say words or sentences loudly, quietly, angrily, or sadly can be a good way for them to explore the power of their voices. The children need to see that you are enthusiastic about dramatizing and enjoy doing the activities you propose. You serve as a model, and encourage them to be active in the classroom.

Organize the classroom

The children stand up in most of the activities, and usually the space at the front of the classroom is enough. If the children stand in a circle or work in groups you need more space: push the tables and chairs to the edge of the classroom, or take the children to the gym. If you use drama activities often, train your children to move the tables and chairs quietly to one side. Give each child one thing to move and practise a few times: make it a competition, they should be as fast and as quiet as possible! If you have real space problems, puppets may be a solution.

Give feedback

You are not training professional actors and actresses but giving children an enjoyable way of practising and using their English. You need to give feedback on what the children have done, not only the end product and language, but also the process that they went through, the way they co-operated with each other, and how they came to decisions. Find something positive to comment on. There will be areas of the children's work that can be improved and this should be part of your feedback to them. While the children are doing the activity, watch and listen to them, try not to interfere, and take notes on what you are observing. The process is your main aim, but the children will see the 'performance' as the most important part of the lesson. You need to value their performances. When they have finished, you can ask some groups to show their work and then give them feedback. There are many ways of doing this: you could prepare a feedback sheet for them to do (see 'Reflection and Feedback', page 96) and use this. If constructive feedback becomes a regular part of dramatization activities, the children will gradually improve their dramatizing abilities and their language.

How to use this book

In this book, you will find drama activities which you can use in the children's classroom to activate language and have fun. The book is divided into six chapters. The first chapter contains guided activities which are important first steps to introducing drama into lesson time and are useful with children who have just started to learn English. Chapter 2 contains advice on using chants, rhymes, and songs. Chapters 3 and 4 are on making and using puppets, and Chapter 5 is about putting on simple plays. In the final chapter the book moves on to role play and improvisation, where children have to use all their language resource creatively. Children, at all language levels, have the opportunity to add something of themselves to these activities using their bodies, voices, and emotions to make the language their own.

How each activity is organized

Level

1 = beginners: from children with little or no knowledge of English, to those who recognize the English names of colours; numbers up to twelve, and basic vocabulary such as the family, animals, some food; *I am/you are*, *there is/there are*, *can*, *like/don't like*; and classroom commands such as *stand up*, *sit down*, and *open your books*. Their active use of this language will be very limited.

2 = elementary: these children are able to use level 1 language more actively and make simple sentences and questions. They have a wider range of vocabulary: for example, clothes, shops, parts of the body, verbs for daily routines, and telling the time in English (if they know this in their own language).

3 = pre-intermediate: these children will be more capable of recognizing sentence patterns and generating language of their own. They are ready to learn structures such as the past simple, comparatives, possibly *going to*, and functions such as obligation, requests, or making suggestions.

It is very important not to confuse these levels with years of English, as a child's maturity makes a great difference to what he or she is able to do. An older child may reach level 2 in one year, while younger children need to go more slowly.

Age group

The letters A, B, and C refer to children's ages:

A = 6–8 years old

B = 8–10 years old

C = 10–12 years old

This is a rough guide only. You must use your own judgement.

Time

A rough guide to how long the activity will take. This will vary considerably according to such factors as the size of the class, the age of the children, whether they are used to working in groups, and so on.

Aims

The aims of the activities are divided into two parts: 'language' aims and 'other' aims. The language aims cover language and skills development, while the others refer to the intellectual and social development of the children.

Description

A short summary of the activity so that you can get an overall idea of it.

Materials

A list of what you need in order to do the activity.

Preparation

A brief outline of what you need to do before the lesson.

In class

A step-by-step guide to doing the activity.

Follow-up

Ideas for further activities which reinforce what has been learnt.

Variations

Examples of ways in which you could adapt the activity to suit your children.

Comments

Hints and advice to make the activity run more smoothly.

1 Getting started

The activities in this chapter allow you to introduce an element of dramatization in your day-to-day lessons and work on the skills necessary for longer activities. They are short, fun, easy to set up, and can be adapted for use with different language content. Many of the activities focus on mime so that children can work on using their bodies to express meaning. This change in focus can be very powerful for language learning: the children acquire the language at a more subconscious level because they are not thinking about what they are saying, but how to show the meaning.

In all the activities, the children work in pairs, groups, or together as a whole class, preparing mimes or mini-sketches. If your children are not used to working in pairs and taking responsibility for their work, you will need to introduce the idea step by step, giving them teacher-controlled activities like 1.1, 'Mime a monster' before moving on to freer work like 1.9, 'Story stills'. Feedback on how the children work together is important to help them learn to work in groups.

If you use these kinds of activities a lot, the children will become comfortable with dramatizing. If you wish to be more ambitious and work on a short play, these introductory activities are an essential bridging point between 'reading the text' and 'acting it out'.

1.1 Mime a monster

LEVEL	1, 2
AGE GROUP	**All**
TIME	**15 minutes**
AIMS	**Language:** vocabulary of parts of the body and listening for detail. **Other:** working in pairs; working on physical co-ordination.
DESCRIPTION	The children work in pairs or groups. The teacher describes a monster which the children make between them with their bodies.
PREPARATION	Prepare the descriptions of the monsters. For example: *Make a monster with two heads, three arms, one leg, and a tail.*
IN CLASS	1 Point at the various parts of the body which you are going to use and elicit the names to check that the children are familiar with them.

2 Ask for two volunteers to come to the front of the class. Explain that they are going to work together to make a monster according to your instructions.

3 Describe the monster and help the volunteers make it with their arms, legs, and other parts of their bodies. Ask for comments from the class and give positive feedback that will help the other children when they are making the monsters.

4 Repeat the activity with the whole class.

5 Note the pairs who have made interesting monsters. Get them to show their monsters to the rest of the class.

FOLLOW-UP

Get the children to draw pictures of the monsters and make a gallery or a 'monster catalogue'.

VARIATION

The children work in groups of three or four to make a monster. One child in each group gives instructions which the others follow. The teacher looks around the class, describes one of the monsters, and the other children identify it.

1.2   Who am I?

LEVEL

1

AGE GROUP

A, B

TIME

15 minutes

AIMS

Language: to revise phrases from the coursebook.
Other: to encourage children to work together in pairs, to work on co-ordination, and encourage children to revise language in their coursebook.

DESCRIPTION

The children work in pairs to represent the characters on a particular page in their book. Each pair shows their mime to the rest of the class, who guess the characters and try to remember what they were saying at the time.

MATERIALS

Your coursebook.

PREPARATION

Prepare a simple mime of a memorable scene in the coursebook.

IN CLASS

1 Ask the children the names of the characters in their book, including animals, robots, witches, and so on!

2 Show the children your mime. Ask them who you are. Can they remember what the character was saying at the time?

3 Tell the children they are going to work in pairs to prepare a mime from the book. Put them into pairs or threes and give them time

to look back through their book, choose a scene, and prepare it. It doesn't need to be static, they can add movement if they want to.

4 When most of the pairs are ready, stop the preparation and ask some groups to show their scene. The other children should guess who they are and what their characters were saying.

FOLLOW-UP

You, or a child, can take photos of the scenes. The children can add speech bubbles to the photos and display them on the wall.

1.3 Statues

LEVEL

1

AGE GROUP

A, B

TIME

15 minutes

AIMS

Language: to revise vocabulary.
Other: to encourage children to work together in pairs, stimulate imagination and creativity, and work on physical co-ordination.

DESCRIPTION

The children work in pairs to mime a word from a 'word family' they have worked on, for example: *pencil*, *pen*, and *pencil case*. They show it to the rest of the class who guess what it is.

IN CLASS

1 Introduce the idea of word families. You could ask the children to tell you the topics they have been working on lately and get them to give you words they associate with the topics, for example: *car*, *train*, and *bus*. Alternatively, you may like to write a few words from each topic and ask the children to group them into families, giving the reasons for their grouping.

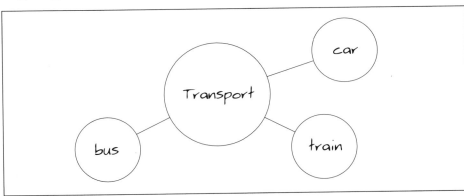

2 Choose a word from one of the families on the board. Tell the children you are going to become a statue of one of the words, and tell them which family it comes from. Mime the word and let the children guess which word it is.

3 Divide the children into pairs. Tell them to select a word from one of the word families on the board.

4 Give the children a few minutes to prepare their statue. Go around the class helping and encouraging.

5 Stop the preparation. Get the pairs to show their statue to the class and get them to guess what it is. If any of the children are really unwilling to show their statue, don't force them.

VARIATION

The children could work in threes or fours to make their statues.

1.4 Find your partner

LEVEL

1, 2

AGE GROUP

A, B

TIME

15 + 15, **including revision of dialogue**

AIMS

Language: to practise vocabulary of feelings and to practise a short dialogue.
Other: to practise showing emotion with voices, faces, and bodies.

DESCRIPTION

The children work on short dialogues (2–4 lines) which they have been studying, and are given a card which tells them how they feel. They mingle with the others in the class, trying to find another person who feels the same way as they do.

MATERIALS

Small cards, each with one of these words on them: *happy*, *sad*, *angry*, *bored*, *hungry*, *tired*, *hot*, and *cold* (see Worksheet 1.4). There should be enough to go around the class, and at least two of each card: it does not matter if there is an uneven number.

PREPARATION

1 Prepare the cards above.

2 Prepare the dialogue you want the children to practise. It can be based on the unit of the book you are doing, or revise something from a previous one. It could be connected with a topic. Or if you are preparing a play to perform, you can use a key dialogue.

IN CLASS

1 Review the dialogue you are going to use. It can be as simple as:
   A *Hi!*
   B *Hello!*
   A *Do you like the new teacher?*
   B *Yes!*

2 For ideas on learning and reviewing dialogues, see pages 93 and 94 in Chapter 5.

3 Present or elicit the feelings that are on the cards you have prepared. You can do this through mime and using your voice, asking *How do I feel?*, or using the pictures in Worksheet 1.4. If these words are new to your children, you may want to write them on the board.

4 Tell the children to work in pairs and choose one of the feelings words. Ask them to practise the dialogue they have learnt, saying it in the manner of the word they have chosen. Go around the class monitoring and commenting. If there is time, they can choose another word and repeat the dialogue using the new word.

5 You may like to ask some of the children to demonstrate their dialogues and ask the class to guess which feeling they are acting. This can be an alternative to step 6 if you don't have enough space for a mingling activity.

6 Give out the cards. Tell the children that they are going to act as if that is how they are feeling at the moment. Explain that they should mingle with the rest of the class, finding partners and saying the dialogue in the manner of their word, until they find someone who feels the same as they do. When they have found a partner, they should stand at the front of the class. If there is an uneven number of children, tell them that there will be one group of three. If you have a large group, it is best to divide the class in two. Let one group do the activity while the others watch, and then let the second group have a turn.

7 When all the children have found a partner, ask some pairs to say the dialogue while the rest of the class guess the feeling.

8 Give the children feedback on the activity, both the language they have been using, and the way in which they carried out the activity.

COMMENTS

If you want a more structured mingling, get the children to stand in two concentric circles, those on the inside facing those on the outside. The children move in opposite directions until you say *stop*. The children facing each other say the dialogue. If their feelings coincide, they leave the circle.

VARIATION 1

Instead of a set dialogue, each child can prepare a question to ask in the manner of the word.

VARIATION 2

Children who are more fluent in English can be asked to improvise using an initial question such as *Where are you going?*

1.5   The multi-purpose spoon

LEVEL

All

AGE GROUP

All

TIME

10 minutes

AIMS

Language: to revise and practise present continuous, *can*, past simple, or other structures.

Other: to encourage children to use their imaginations and to practise using a simple prop.

DESCRIPTION

The children work as a class or in large groups. They sit or stand in a circle and pass the spoon around. Each child uses the spoon to represent an action. The others guess what they are doing.

MATERIALS

One wooden spoon for each group of 8–10 children or one 'multi-purpose object' (for example: a box, paper plate, or newspaper) for each group of 8–10 children.

PREPARATION

1 Choose the structure you want to work on.
2 Think of how to contextualize the structure.
3 Decide on a simple action using the spoon to show the class.

IN CLASS

1 Show the children a wooden spoon (or other multi-purpose object). Give a short introduction to contextualize the structure you want to practise. For example: *I'm going to use this spoon to tell you what I did at the weekend.* Use it to mime an action and at the same time say the sentence using the structure you want to practise. For example, pretend to hit a ball, use the spoon as a tennis racket, and say: *I played tennis at the weekend.*

2 Ask the children to think of other things they could use the spoon to show. When a child has an idea, give them the spoon so that they can show the class. Ask the other children to guess the sentence.

3 When the children have understood the activity, divide them into groups of about ten and get each group to stand (or sit) in a circle. Give each group a spoon. Explain that the children should take turns to use the spoon to act out something and the others should guess the sentence. You may like to say that the spoon should go around the circle at least twice.

4 When most of the groups have finished, stop the activity and ask them to sit down. The groups should now try to remember what each person did. With children who have a higher level of English this can be done in pairs or small groups, or there could be a group secretary who writes down the sentences as the whole group tries to remember.

VARIATION

With older children: you can turn the activity into a competition by asking each group to read out its sentences. As the sentences are read out to the whole class, the group secretary should cross any sentences off the list that are the same. The children then count the sentences that remain on the list: the group with the largest number of original sentences is the winner.

FOLLOW-UP

Each group makes a poster of its original sentences. The teacher makes a poster of the sentences the groups had in common.

1.6 Listen and mime

LEVEL	**All**
AGE GROUP	**All**
TIME	**15–30 minutes, depending on the story**
AIMS	**Language:** to listen to a story and listen for specific words and phrases. **Other:** to use actions to illustrate a story.
DESCRIPTION	The children listen to a story, and do actions as they hear certain words.
MATERIALS	A story, for example, 'Enormous Elephant' on pages 20–21.

PREPARATION

1 Choose a story and write a story skeleton for it.
2 Practise telling it, to a colleague if possible.
3 Select key words from the story and think of gestures to illustrate them.
4 Practise telling the story, making the gestures at the same time.

IN CLASS

Before the story

1 Tell the children that you are going to tell them a story, but that they need to learn some actions first.
2 Ask the children to stand up, in a circle if possible. Join them in the circle: start by teaching them two or three words and actions. Then repeat the words in a different order and get the children to do the actions (they don't need to say the words).
3 Teach a few more words and actions. Get the children to do the actions for the new words and old words mixed together. Continue adding a few more words and actions one at a time until you have presented and practised them all.

EXAMPLE

Words for miming	Actions
Enormous	*Starting above your head, trace a big circle with your hands*
Elephant	*Wave an arm in front of your nose like an elephant's trunk*
bored	*Put your head in your hand with bored expression on your face*
idea	*Point at your head with a sudden, pleased expression on your face*
walk	*Walk a few steps on the spot*
New York	*Put both hands above your head to make a skyscraper*
meet	*Turn to someone beside you and shake hands*

Magic	*Hold up your hands and shimmer them down like magic dust*
Monkey	*Scratch your head with one hand and under one arm with another*
What's the matter?	*Open your hands and shrug your shoulders in a questioning way*
OK	*The usual gesture in your country for OK*
Crazy	*The usual gesture in your country for crazy*
Crocodile	*Make snapping crocodile jaws with outstretched arms*
tired	*Sag your body*
sleep	*Put your head on your two hands*

STORY OUTLINE

ENORMOUS ELEPHANT

This is the story of Enormous Elephant, Magic Monkey, and Crazy Crocodile.

One day Enormous Elephant was bored, very very bored. Then he had an idea.

'I know,' he said, 'I'll go to New York.'

So he started to walk, and he walked, and he walked, and he walked. On the way he met Magic Monkey.

'Hello, Magic Monkey,' he said.

'Hello,' said Magic Monkey.

'What's the matter?' said Enormous Elephant.

'I'm bored,' said Magic Monkey, 'very, very bored.'

'I've got an idea,' said Enormous Elephant, 'why don't you come to New York with me?'

'OK,' said Magic Monkey.

So they started to walk, and they walked, and they walked, and they walked. On the way they met Crazy Crocodile.

'Hello, Crazy Crocodile,' they said.

'Hello,' said Crazy Crocodile.

'What's the matter?' said Enormous Elephant.

'I'm bored,' said Crazy Crocodile, 'very, very bored.'

'I've got an idea,' said Enormous Elephant, 'why don't you come to New York with us?'

'OK,' said Crazy Crocodile.

So they started to walk, and they walked, and walked, and walked.

And they walked, and they walked, and they walked.

And they walked, and they walked, and they walked.

'Oh, I'm tired,' said Enormous Elephant.

'Oh, I'm tired,' said Magic Monkey.

'Oh, I'm tired,' said Crazy Crocodile.

So they all went to sleep.

Telling the story

4 Ask the children to stand up, and make sure they can all see you. Again, a circle is the best option if possible. Elicit the actions if you have taught them in an earlier lesson. Ask the children to listen to the story and do the appropriate action each time they hear one of the words you have been practising.

5 Tell the story, doing the actions as you tell it. Encourage the children to join in the actions with you.

6 Tell the story again, in this or a later class. On subsequent tellings you may feel that you don't need to model the actions.

Acknowledgement

I learnt this story from a colleague, Guy Norman, who learned it at an APIGA conference some 10 years ago. I would like to acknowledge the unknown author of this most successful story.

FOLLOW-UP

You can do a variety of follow-ups after telling a story with actions:

- make a comic strip or book of the story;
- give the written story with gaps for the words with actions;
- ask them to put pictures of the story in order, and write a sentence for each one;
- ask them to think of a variation on the story;
- show the story to an audience. You could add masks, hats, and so on (see Chapter 3).

There are many ideas for using stories in the young learners' classroom in *Storytelling with Children* by Andrew Wright.

VARIATIONS

- If the words are familiar, show the children the actions and ask them to guess what the words might be.
- Present the words through pictures and then ask the children to invent the actions for the words themselves.
- Ask the children to predict the story from the words with actions.
- With a story with three or four main characters, divide the children into small groups, one for each character, and get them to do the actions as you tell it.

COMMENTS

You may like to do the 'before story' activity in one or more lessons before you tell the story. Many authentic children's stories of the kind that build up by repeating a basic structure lend themselves to this kind of activity. For example: *The Elephant and The Bad Baby and The Enormous Turnip* (see Further Reading, page 149).

1.7   What am I telling you?

LEVEL	**All**
AGE GROUP	**All**
TIME	**15 minutes**
AIMS	**Language:** to revise and recycle language from previous lessons. **Other:** to practise communicating without words and to encourage children to look for alternatives when their first guess is wrong.
DESCRIPTION	Two children mime a sentence and the other children guess what the sentence is.
MATERIALS	Pre-prepared sentences on slips of paper (see examples below).
PREPARATION	Prepare some sentences connected with the topic or language point you are working on or want to revise. It is best to set the sentences in a context—in a restaurant, at the police station, on a radio phone-in show, or from a story or song. Remember, it must be possible to mime the sentences. There are some examples in the box below.

EXAMPLES

In a restaurant

Waiter, can I have the menu, please?
I'd like some spaghetti.
Can we have some fresh orange juice?
This steak is tough.

From a story

The princess had long hair and blue eyes.
She dropped her ball into a pond.
The frog swam to the bottom of the pond and found the ball.
The princess didn't want to kiss the frog.

A situation: in the supermarket

He's buying some apples.
The bananas are cheap.
Where are the ice creams?

IN CLASS

1 Set the context for the situation you have chosen, perhaps through pictures on the board or by miming. For example, if you've chosen 'in the supermarket', you could draw pictures of food, or you could mime buying something.

2 Show the children the sentence slips and choose one that is very easy to mime. Ask for two volunteers to come and read it silently. Make sure the children understand the sentence, helping them if necessary.

3 Tell the class that the volunteers are going to 'tell' the other children what is on the slip without speaking, writing, or drawing. Ask the other children how the volunteers could do this.

4 Ask the volunteers to have a go, either individually or together (see Comments).

5 When the class has guessed the sentence, or close to it, it is useful to get them to think about their classmates' performance. This reflection will help them when they try miming themselves. Ask them to say two things they liked about the performance and one thing that could be improved. Tell the children to remember those things when it is their turn. If you think it is necessary, do the same thing with another two volunteers.

6 When you think the class is ready to work in small groups, divide the children into groups of four or five. Tell them that two children from each group should come to you to collect a sentence to mime. When the group has guessed the sentence, two more children should come to you. They must tell you the sentence they have just guessed before you give them another one.

7 End the activity when each group has guessed five or six sentences.

COMMENTS	Before the volunteers try to mime the sentence (step 4), you may like to work as a class on a series of helpful gestures. For example, a gesture to represent the number of words in the sentence could involve holding up the number of fingers. Other instructions could tell the class which word the child is miming or if the words are long or short. On the other hand, you may like to let the volunteers try to mime the sentence first, and then get the children to think how they could have made the sentence clearer.
FOLLOW-UP 1	Ask each group to choose one mime they would like to show to the class.
FOLLOW-UP 2	Ask the children to remember and write down the sentences they have mimed.
FOLLOW-UP 3	Ask the children to work some of the sentences into a dialogue.
VARIATION 1	When the class is used to doing the activity, the children themselves can think of the sentences to be mimed. You may like to turn the activity into a team game.
VARIATION 2	The children can mouth the words as well as miming them.

1.8   Who are we?

LEVEL	2, 3
AGE GROUP	**B, C**
TIME	**Either 3 x 15-minute slots in different lessons, or 15–30 minutes preparing and 15 minutes presentation.**
AIMS	**Language:** to revise and recycle language from previous lessons. **Other:** to think about and use appropriate gestures, body language, and voice to represent character and to think about staging (entrances, exits, movements) in a short sketch
DESCRIPTION	The children work in groups of two or three to prepare a sketch involving a conversation between a group of characters, including, for example, 'an old person' or 'a person in a hurry'. The class watches the sketch and guesses who the characters are.
MATERIALS	Cards with the characters written on them like the ones in the box (these can be in the children's first language); space in the room.
PREPARATION	1 Choose a simple dialogue that you want the children to work on. Decide on where the conversation takes place, for example: in the street, or in a bar. If your children are more fluent, you can simply choose a situation and let them improvise the conversation. See the examples of a conversation and situation below:
EXAMPLES	

A conversation that takes place in the street

A Excuse me! Where's the park?
B It's over there.
A Where? I can't see it.
B Look where I'm pointing. Over there, near the river!

A situation where the children improvise the conversation

It's Saturday afternoon. One person wants to watch television. Another person wants to go out and play football. The third person wants some peace and quiet.

---

2 Prepare cards with characters written on them (see 'Suggestions for characters'). You need a card for each child but the characters can be duplicated, for a class of 24, eight characters are enough.

EXAMPLES

> **Suggestions for characters**
> A deaf person
> A person in a hurry
> A person with a broken arm
> A person with a broken leg
> A person with a bad cold
> An old person
> A person carrying a lot of shopping
> A child on a skateboard
> A child on roller skates
> A very tired person
> A person with a dog
> A person in a bad mood

IN CLASS

Preparing the children for their sketch

This may need a whole lesson.

1 If the children are not used to acting out different characters, you can start by helping them get 'inside' a character. Write up one of the characters on your cards on the board.

2 Help the children to think about his or her physical appearance. Draw, or ask the children to draw, a picture of the character on the board. Then ask the children to use their imagination and show you how the character stands, walks, holds their head, and so on.

3 Help the children to identify with the character's personality like this: draw a thought bubble coming from the character's head. If the character is tired or bad-tempered you can ask the children why they feel like this. Ask the children what they think the character is thinking and feeling.

4 Ask all the children to stand up and become the character. Comment on the gestures and actions they use and encourage them to be as creative as possible.

5 Ask them to say their name in the way the character would. Comment on how they use their voices.

Practising the sketch

6 Write the characters you have chosen on the board. Tell the children that they are each going to become one of the characters. You may like to repeat steps 1, 2, and 3 if you feel the class need help in identifying with their character.

7 Give out the cards and ask the children to imagine being their character.

8 Teach or elicit the conversation if you are using one.

9 Tell the children the situation, for example, 'On a bus'. You may like to arrange some desks and chairs to set the scene, and get the children to help. Keep it very simple. Make sure the entrances and exits are well defined—for example, doors in a room, streets coming on to a square, the front door of a house.

10 Put the children in pairs or small groups. Give them plenty of time to work on the conversation. Remind them that they should use the space, not simply stand still in the middle of it. As they work, circulate and comment on their sketches.

Performing the sketch

11 In this or a different lesson, ask some of the groups to show their sketches. The rest of the class guesses who they are.

12 Give feedback on the performances. Ask the children what they liked and how the performances could be improved. (For more on feedback, see 'Reflection and feedback', page 96.)

13 If you are going to do this activity regularly, and it is appropriate, make a poster of the positive points and the suggestions the children have made. They can refer to it the next time you do the activity.

COMMENTS

If your children are new to this kind of activity, part 1 'Preparing the children for their sketch', will probably take a whole lesson. If you are preparing a play, you can use this activity to help the children to work on developing their roles, and learning their lines.

VARIATIONS

- If you have access to a video camera, you can video the scenes instead of the groups giving performances.

- The children can write the dialogues or a description of the scene.

1.9 Story stills

LEVEL	2, 3
AGE GROUP	C
TIME	**45 minutes**
AIMS	**Language:** to listen to a story and use language of discussion and negotiation. **Other:** to work together co-operatively in small groups; to focus on the physical composition of a scene using body language and gesture.
DESCRIPTION	The children listen to a story. Then they prepare scenes for key points in the story, 'freeze-framed', as if they were stills from a film. The teacher or a child could take photos of their stills to be displayed in the classroom.
MATERIALS	Paper and coloured pencils, scissors, a camera.
PREPARATION	1 Choose a suitable story; ideally it should have four or five principal characters and a flexible number of extra characters. It also needs to have four or five well-defined points in the story suitable for representing as stills. 2 Practise drawing stills and making paper figures.
IN CLASS	**In the first lesson** 1 Introduce the characters and tell the story. This may be the story of a play like the ones in Chapter 5, or ones like those in *Storytelling with Children* by Andrew Wright.

In another lesson

2 Elicit and review the story and make a list of the principal characters on the board.

3 Draw four or five (depending on possibilities for stills in the story) film-style frames on the board. Tell the children that these are for pictures that represent the story.

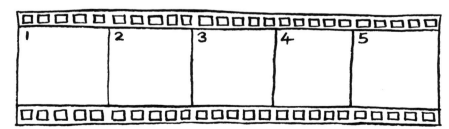

4 Ask the children which points of the story the pictures could illustrate. At the bottom of each picture frame write a title and the names of the characters that appear in that frame.

5 Ask the children to imagine the background to each frame. Sketch in their suggestions, or ask one of the children to draw for you.

6 Divide the class into groups; each group should have at least one child for each character in the story. If there are uneven numbers, the other children can be extras.

7 Tell the groups that they are going to plan stills of the frames they have described. Ask them to draw the film frames as you have done. Show them how to cut out paper figures and arrange them.

8 When they are satisfied with their pictures, ask them to find a space and make a tableau of one of the scenes. Remind them that you will be taking photos of them when they have finished. Give them the deadline—it may be in this or a subsequent lesson.

9 When the groups are ready they show their stills to the class. You, or one of the children, can take photos of the work. These can be mounted to make posters and displayed alongside the pictures made with cut-out figures.

FOLLOW-UP

There are a number of possible follow-ups to this activity:

- the children write captions for the photos;
- they can write speech or thought bubbles for the photos;
- they can use them to illustrate a written version of the story.

If you don't have access to a camera, you could end the activity by getting the groups to display their stills while the rest of the class guess which part of the story it comes from.

2 Songs, rhymes, and chants

Songs and rhymes provide a rich source of texts for acting out. They are especially useful in classes of younger children who may not be able to produce much of their own language. Rhythm and melody make language easier to learn and remember, and movement and gesture help illustrate meaning. Songs appeal to the whole child through visual, aural, and kinaesthetic (physical) channels. Songs, rhymes, and chants can be used as the first steps to a more independent kind of acting. By providing children with the words, we leave them free to concentrate on expressing feelings and character through body language and gesture. Later, as they become more confident and aware of the possibilities of their own bodies, they are able to use their own words.

You will often find that the instructions fall into two parts. In the first part, the children learn the words and actions to the song or chant as a whole class. In the second, they work in small groups on a version of their own: they may personalize it by changing the actions, or by adapting the text. It is usually best that these two parts fall in different lessons. The time between lessons allows the language to 'sink in' and become assimilated, before actions and rhyme are added.

Both teachers and children vary in the amount of control they want to have over an activity. As a teacher, it is sometimes difficult to let the children have a free hand in what they are doing, and some children find total freedom of decision difficult to cope with. You need to decide what balance you feel comfortable with, and work towards it step by step.

2.1 Conduct a chant

LEVEL	**All**
AGE GROUP	**All**
TIME	**10–15 minutes**
AIMS	**Language:** to practise stress and rhythm. **Other:** to practise chanting in chorus, work on communication through gesture and group dynamics.

DESCRIPTION

The children learn a short chant and say it in chorus. They invent gestures to control the speed and volume of their words and work in groups to prepare a 'concert' performance.

MATERIALS

If you want the children to practise reading, make large cards, each with one word or phrase of the chant.

PREPARATION

Prepare the word cards if you are going to use them.

IN CLASS

1 Draw a robot on the board and ask the children what it is, and how it moves and talks.

2 Ask the children to mime these actions like a robot:

Rhyme word	*Actions*
think	*Lift arm stiffly and point to head*
drink	*Mime lifting a cup to your mouth in two sudden movements*
walk	*Walk with straight legs and arms*
talk	*Talk with a mechanical voice*
write	*Mime writing with stiff movements*
fight	*Lift fists and punch the air with stiff movements*
hop	*Stand on one leg and jump into the air with very straight arms and legs*
stop	*Stop very suddenly*

3 Say the rhyme and encourage the children to do the actions. Then say it line by line and get them to repeat it after you.

We are robots

● · ● ·
We are robots

● · ● ·
We are robots

● · ● ·
Robots thinking

● · ● ·
Robots drinking

● · ● ·
Robots walking

● · ● ·
Robots talking

● · ● ·
We are robots

● · ● ·
We are robots

● · ● ·
Robots writing

● · ● ·
Robots fighting

● · ● ·
Robots hopping

● · ● ·
Robots stopping

● · ● ·
We are robots

● · ● ·
We are robots

4 If you have made word cards of the poem (see materials), give them out to the class, one to each child. Ask who has the first word, then the next, and so on. The children can stick their words on the board or come to the front of the class and hold them up in the right order.

5 When the children know the rhyme, get them to say it slowly, quickly, loudly, quietly, and in combinations; for example, starting slowly and getting faster, or starting quietly and getting louder.

6 Ask the children if they know how a conductor controls an orchestra. Ask them what hand signals you could use to tell them you want them to go slowly, quickly, loudly, and quietly. Practise them with the children and then ask them if they think the gestures are clear, or if they want to change them.

7 Ask a few children to take turns conducting the class. Comment on their gestures making it clear that the gestures need to be large, deliberate, and without abrupt changes.

8 Ask each group to prepare a 'concert'. When the groups are ready they can perform their version for the rest of the class.

| COMMENTS | The technique can be used with any short rhyme or chant, for example 'Coffee, coffee' in *Young Learners* (see Further reading), as well as when preparing other rhymes and chants in this section. |

2.2 Five little monkeys

LEVEL	1
AGE GROUP	A, B
TIME	**20 minutes**
AIMS	**Language:** to work on the stress and rhythm of spoken English and practise recognition of isolated words embedded in a text. **Other:** Total Physical Response and group co-ordination.
DESCRIPTION	The children say and act out a traditional rhyme.
MATERIALS	A blackboard and space in the classroom. You could use some simple props, for example: a toy stethoscope, doctor's glasses, and a toy telephone.
PREPARATION	1 Learn the chant. 2 Practise drawing the picture.

Five little monkeys

•   •   •   •   •   •   •   •

Five little monkeys jumping on the bed

•   •   •   •   •   •

One fell off and bumped his head

•   •   •   • •   •   •   • •   •

Mummy phoned the doctor and the doctor said

•   •   •   •   •   •   •

'No more jumping on the bed!'

Continue with:

Four little monkeys
Three little monkeys
Two little monkeys
One little monkey

IN CLASS

Learning the chant

1 Copy the picture onto the board and tell the children that you are
going to teach them a story about five little monkeys. Show them
the monkeys on the bed, Mummy, the phone, and the doctor.

2 Ask the children if they have ever jumped on the bed (you can do
this in their own language). What might happen? Has anyone
fallen off? Check key vocabulary: *monkey, jump, bed, head,
Mummy, phone, doctor.*

3 Teach the children the first two lines, miming as you do so.
Encourage the children to join in the actions, and the words too if
they want to.

4 Ask the children how Mummy feels and what they think she will
do next. What will the doctor do and say? Ask them to act out
their suggestions.

5 Teach the children the last two lines, mime a worried Mummy
and a severe doctor shaking his finger at the monkey who has
fallen off.

6 Repeat the rhyme with four monkeys, and so on.

Performing the chant

7 Remind the children of the rhyme. Chant the first verse together.

8 Divide the children into groups of seven (five monkeys, Mummy, and the doctor). If your class does not divide into groups of seven, you can add other characters—Daddy, a nurse, a brother, or sister. Substitute these characters for Mummy in some verses of the rhyme.

9 Make sure each group has a space to work in. Draw a rectangle on the floor with chalk to represent the bed for each group. Tell the children they are going to act out the poem. Give them time to practise.

10 Each individual group acts out their version of the chant while the whole class chants the poem.

11 Give the children feedback on their performance, balancing good points and points to be improved. You may like to ask the children to evaluate their own performance too.

2.3 I'm big, I'm small

LEVEL	1
AGE GROUP	**A, B**
TIME	**20 minutes to learn the poem; 20 minutes to prepare the presentation (in a different lesson).**
AIMS	**Language:** to present and practise adjectives (*big, small, short, tall, good, bad, happy, sad*). **Other:** to encourage children to associate adjectives with movement and work on group dynamics.
DESCRIPTION	The children act out a poem.
PREPARATION	1 Learn the poem.

I'm big, I'm small

. •
I'm big.
. •
I'm small.
. •
I'm short.
. •
I'm tall.
. •
I'm happy.
. •
I'm sad.
. •
I'm good.

I'm bad.
We're friends.
That's the end.

I'm big.   I'm small.   I'm short.   I'm tall.   I'm happy.   I'm sad.

I'm good.   I'm bad.   We're friends. That's the end.

2 Practise the drawings.

IN CLASS

Learning the poem

1 Use board drawings like those in the illustration to teach the adjectives.

2 Ask the children to suggest an action or mime for each adjective.

3 Get the children to do the actions as you call out the adjectives.

4 Draw a speech bubble coming out of one character's mouth. Write *I'm big* in it. Draw speech bubbles for the rest of the characters and ask the children what they are saying. Write the words in the bubbles.

5 Ask the children to stand up. Say the first eight lines of the poem together, doing the actions as you go.

I'm big.
I'm small.
I'm short.
I'm tall.
I'm happy.
I'm sad.
I'm good.
I'm bad.

6 Teach them the last two lines and ask them to think of an action or mime for these lines.

We're friends.
That's the end.

7 Say the poem and do the actions again.

Acting out the poem

1 Elicit the poem, say it, and do the actions together.

2 Divide the children into groups of four or eight. Tell them that you want them to act out the poem. At this point, you can either give the children guidance or let them work independently. This will depend on both the age of the children and their experience of working alone. In either case they need to decide:
  – who says which part of the poem (one line each? all together?);
  – how they are going to stand (in a row? in a circle?);
  – if they are going to move (taking steps forward and backwards? in a circle?);
  – how the poem starts and ends.

3 Give the children 10–15 minutes to practise their presentation. While they are working, go around the class, encouraging and helping where necessary. Give your honest opinion of what they have done. If you say you like it, help them to reflect on their work by asking them why they think you like it.

FOLLOW-UP	– Ask one or more groups to show their poem to the class. – The children draw their own pictures for the poem.
VARIATION 1	You can make this activity more challenging and creative with older children. Start by presenting the first four lines of the poem, and then brainstorm other adjectives for describing people and their feelings (*old, young, hot, cold, dirty, clean, kind, mean*). Ask the children to add another four or eight lines to the poem. Get them to prepare the presentation as above.
VARIATION 2	Vary the person of the poem, using *you, he, she, we,* or *they.* The actions in the presentation must make the meaning of the subject pronoun clear.

2.4 Two tall daddies

LEVEL	1, 2
AGE GROUP	**A, B**
TIME	**20 minutes in the first lesson; 20 minutes in the second.**
AIMS	**Language:** to recognize sounds and rhythms of English and vocabulary of the family.

Other: Total Physical Response, using different kinds of voices, and co-ordinating in groups and pairs.

DESCRIPTION

The children learn a poem. Pairs of children take different roles in the poem and do simple actions as the class recites it.

MATERIALS

None, though you may like to use simple finger puppets with the poem (see 3.3).

PREPARATION

1 Learn the poem yourself.
2 Decide how the children are going to act it out, and what actions they will do.
3 Prepare pictures of the tall daddies, busy mummies, and other characters.

Two tall daddies

Words	Suggested actions
• · • ·	
Two tall daddies	*Stand on tip toes and walk around being 'tall'*
• · • ·	
Walking down the lane	*March in one direction*
• · • ·	
Waved to each other	*Wave*
• · • · •	
And then they waved again	*Wave again*
• · •	
How are you?	*Nod heads*

● · ●
How are you?   *Nod heads again*

● · ●
Lovely day again!   *Point to the sky*

Continue the poem using these phrases instead of 'Two tall daddies':

Two busy mummies
Two best friends
Two noisy sisters
Two little brothers

IN CLASS

Learning the chant

1 Show the children the pictures and introduce the characters.

2 Ask the children to think of an action that represents each character, or show them the ones you have prepared.

3 Say the names of the characters and get the children to do the appropriate action.

4 Say the rhyme and teach it to the children. Chant it two or three times together.

Performing the chant

5 Elicit and review the rhyme and the actions.

6 Divide the children into pairs. Assign a character to each pair. You could put five pairs together to make a group of ten, with all the characters in the poem.

7 The pairs or groups act out the rhyme like this:

The whole class says the first part of the poem, while those in each group or pair who are the 'tall daddies' do the actions:

Everybody	Two tall daddies
	Walking down the lane
	Waved to each other
	And then they waved again
Tall daddy 1	How are you?
Tall daddy 2	How are you?
Daddies together	Lovely day again!

Repeat the verse but each time introduce one of the other characters (mummies, friends, sisters, brothers) into the verse.

8 The whole class practises the poem together two or three times. If you have decided to get the children to work on the poem in groups, they can now practise acting it out on their own. You should go around the class monitoring, helping, and giving feedback.

VARIATION

The adjectives for the characters can be changed, or you may like to ask the children to suggest some.

COMMENTS

There are other well-known songs and poems that you can use for acting out. For example: 'The Wheels on the Bus Go Round and Round', 'Miss Polly Had a Dolly', 'There Were Ten in the Bed', 'Five Little Ducks', 'Five Little Speckled Frogs'. You can find these in books of traditional rhymes, or in the videos *Fun Song Factory 1* and *Fun Song Factory 2*.

2.5 The Marching Band

LEVEL

1, 2

AGE GROUP

A, B

TIME

20 minutes in the first class, 20 minutes in the second.

AIMS

Language: to learn vocabulary of musical instruments.
Other: co-ordination through miming and marching.

DESCRIPTION

The children mime a marching band and sing a song about musical instruments.

MATERIALS

Pictures of musical instruments, a piece of music with different musical instruments on it.

PREPARATION

1 Make pictures of musical instruments (see Worksheet 2.5).

2 If possible, find a recording of a piece of music with various instruments.

The marching band
(Tune: 'Here We Go Round the Mulberry Bush', traditional)

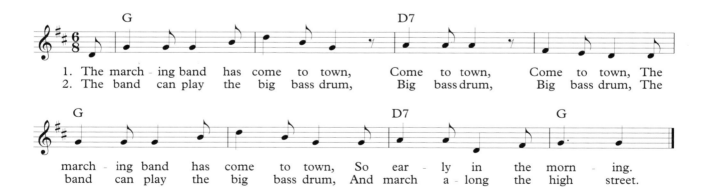

1. The march-ing band has come to town, Come to town, Come to town, The
2. The band can play the big bass drum, Big bass drum, Big bass drum, The

march-ing band has come to town, So ear-ly in the morn-ing.
band can play the big bass drum, And march a-long the high street.

Substitute some or any of these instruments in other verses:

long trombone	silver flute	loud cymbals	piano
triangle	accordion	violin	

IN CLASS

1 Ask if any children can play an instrument, or if they know anyone who can. Ask them the names of musical instruments they know and teach them the English names if necessary. Include the names of the instruments which appear in the song.

2 Get the children to mime how the instruments are played. Children who play instruments can demonstrate.

3 This step is optional: play a piece of music in which different instruments can be clearly heard. Ask the children which instruments they can hear. Get them to mime the instruments as they hear them.

4 Sing the 'Marching Band' song. Ask the children which instruments are in the band in the song. Teach them the adjectives for instruments, for example, long trombone.

5 Sing the song again and ask the children to clap and march on the spot in time to the first and last verses (these are the 'marching band' verse), and to mime the instruments in the others.

6 Teach the children the words of the verses with instruments:

The Band can play the big bass drum
Big bass drum
Big bass drum
The Band can play the big bass drum
And march along the high street

7 Practise singing the song.

8 Ask if any children have seen a marching band, and get them to explain how the band line up. If you can, divide the children into groups of 15 or 16 and stand them in five rows of three, or four rows of four, with a band leader at the front. Practise marching along in time to the first verse.

9 Finally, play and sing the whole song as the band marches and mimes the instruments.

10 The children can add verses with other instruments.

FOLLOW-UP 1

Make hats for the band (see 3.10, 'Hat base' and 3.11, 'Headband').

FOLLOW-UP 2

Make simple percussion instruments and then use these to accompany the band. You can make instruments by putting beans in empty drinks cans or yoghurt pots, stretching paper over old biscuit tins, and hitting wooden or metal spoons together.

FOLLOW-UP 3

Make a frieze of the band to put on the wall.

2.6 Who stole the cookie from the cookie jar?

LEVEL	1, 2
AGE GROUP	A, B
TIME	**25 minutes to learn the chant; 25 minutes to prepare the presentation (in a different lesson).**
AIMS	**Language:** to practise the stress and rhythm of spoken English and take part in a simple question and answer exchange. To listen for key words in a text. **Other:** to express emotions with body language and stimulate imagination.
DESCRIPTION	First, the children learn a traditional chant with a question and answer verse and a chorus. Then they add actions to it. Finally, they suggest new words and actions for their own version.
MATERIALS	Some biscuits in a biscuit jar and a soft toy that you can use to 'steal' some biscuits ('cookies').

PREPARATION

Learn the chant

All	Who stole the cookie from the cookie jar?
Teacher	Maria stole the cookie from the cookie jar.
Maria	Who, me?
Teacher	Yes, you.
Maria	Not me!
Teacher	Then who?
All	Who stole the cookie from the cookie jar?
Maria	Pablo!
All	Pablo stole the cookie from the cookie jar.
Pablo	Who me?
Maria	Yes, you.
Pablo	Not me!
Maria	Then who?
All	Who stole the cookie from the cookie jar?
Pablo	(another child's name)

IN CLASS

Learning the chant

1 Show the children a biscuit jar with some biscuits in it, or draw a picture on the board. Teach them 'cookies' and 'cookie jar'. Tell them that you are Mum or Dad and that they and the soft toy are your children. You are all in the kitchen and the cookie jar contains your favourite cookies.

2 Count the number of cookies. Make the soft toy 'steal' a cookie. Count them again and say the first line of the chant looking indignant, perhaps with your hands on your hips:

● ● · ● · · · ● · ●

Who stole the cookie from the cookie jar?

3 Get the children to repeat the line. Write it on the board.

4 Look at a child (choose one who will enjoy taking part in the play acting) and say:
(Name) stole the cookie from the cookie jar.

Get the children to repeat the line. Write it on the board. Practise the first two lines.

5 Ask the child how he or she feels. Did he or she really steal the cookie? Teach him or her the next line:
Who me?

Get the class to reply:
Yes, you!

and teach the reply:
Not me!

Write these lines on the board.

Practise the chant from the beginning.

6 Teach and practise the next two lines:

Teacher *Then who?*
All   *Who stole the cookie from the cookie jar?*

Write them on the board. Practise the chant from the beginning.

7 Ask the child to accuse someone else and teach the line:

Child *(name)*
All   *(name) stole the cookie from the cookie jar!*

8 Write the line on the board, and draw an arrow back to the first line to show that the chant repeats itself. This time the dialogue is between the first and second child, with the rest of the class chanting the chorus.

> Who stole the cookie from the cookie jar?
> (name) stole the cookie from the cookie jar?
> Who me?
> Yes, you!
> Not me!
> Then who?
> Who stole the cookie from the cookie jar?
> (name)
> (name) stole the cookie from the cookie jar

9 Repeat the chant from the beginning, and as many times with different names as the children wish to. If the children get confused, it is often better to stop the chant and go back to it later.

Performing the chant with mime

10 Ask the children if they have ever been unjustly accused of doing something wrong. How did they feel? How can they show how they felt with their faces and bodies?

11 Remind them of the chant. Remind them that it takes place in the kitchen. What do they think they are doing there (cooking, doing homework, eating, playing). Ask them to mime these activities.

12 Say the chant again, but this time the children include mime and facial expressions.

Adaptation and presentation

13 If necessary, remind the children of the chant and practise it.

14 Ask the children what other things could be stolen and where from, for example, treasure from a treasure chest, apples from the fruit bowl, chocolate from the Christmas tree, washing from the washing line. Write the suggestions on the board.

15 Write *cookie* and *cookie jar* on the board and get the children to clap out the syllables.

Explain that you want to change the words of the chant and that you need to find words that fit the rhythm.

16 Try doing the chant with some of the children's suggestions.

17 Ask the children to imagine who would be asking and answering the questions and for each of their suggested substitutions.

18 If you are working with older children, divide them into groups of four or five. Get each group to choose which substitution they want to work on and ask them to think of mimes for the rhyme. If you are working with younger children you will probably need to work with the whole class on the presentation of the substitution they choose. Ask them for suggestions and help them build up the presentation together.

19 One or two groups can show their version of the rhyme.

COMMENTS

You can give the children numbers, colours, animal names, and so on, instead of their own names.

2.7   The dragon hunt

LEVEL	2, 3
AGE GROUP	B, C
TIME	**25 minutes to learn the poem; 25 minutes to prepare the presentation (in a different lesson).**
AIMS	**Language:** to work on the stress and rhythm of spoken English and revise and reinforce prepositions, plus *can't* for possibility and *must* for obligation. **Other:** to work on body language, group co-ordination, and using imagination.
DESCRIPTION	The children act out a traditional echo chant.
MATERIALS	Flashcards showing two children 'armed' with sticks and a huge net and flashcards showing a dragon, long grass, wet mud, and water (see Worksheet 2.7).
PREPARATION	1 Learn and practise the chant.
	2 This activity is best done in a large open space. If you are in class, push the tables and chairs back in the classroom. If that is not possible, create a space at the front of the classroom.
	3 Decide where these places are in the room: home, the long grass, the wet mud, the water, the cave. They should be on a route arranged so that as large a group of children as possible can follow.

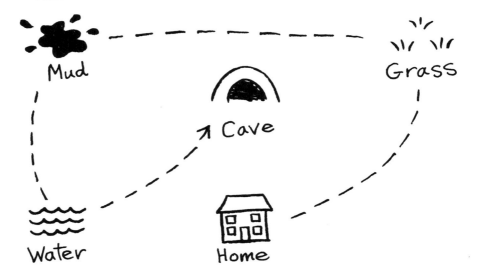

The dragon hunt
(based on *We're Going on a Bear Hunt* by Michael Rosen and Helen Oxenbury, see Further Reading)

Verse 1

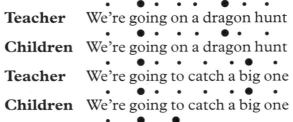

Teacher   We're going on a dragon hunt

Children   We're going on a dragon hunt

Teacher   We're going to catch a big one

Children   We're going to catch a big one

Teacher   We're not scared

Children   We're not scared.

Verse 2

Teacher   Oh no, grass, long green grass

Children   Oh no, grass, long green grass

Teacher   We can't go over it

Children   We can't go over it

Teacher   We can't go under it

Children   We can't go under it

Teacher   We can't go round it

Children   We can't go round it

Teacher   We must go through it

Children   We must go through it.

Together   Swish, swish

Together   Swish, swish, swish.

Continue with:

Verse 3
Oh no, water, cold wet water
Oh no, water, cold wet water
Together
Splash, splash
Splash, splash, splash.

Verse 4
Oh no, mud, black sticky mud
Oh no, mud, black sticky mud
Together
Squelch, squelch
Squelch, squelch, squelch.

Verse 5
Oh look, a cave, a big dark cave
Oh look, a cave, a big dark cave
Chorus
Shh, shh,
Shh, shh, shh

Verse 6
Oh no, a dragon, a fierce fiery dragon
Oh no, a dragon, a fierce fiery dragon
Teacher Quick run
Children Quick run
Teacher Out of the cave
Together Shh, shh
Together Shh, shh, shh
Teacher Through the mud
Together Squelch, squelch
Together Squelch, squelch, squelch
Teacher Through the water
Together Splash, splash
Together Splash, splash, splash
Teacher Through the grass
Together Swish, swish
Together Swish, swish, swish
Teacher And back home
Together Phew!

IN CLASS

1 Show the children the flashcards and see if they can give you the words *grass*, *water*, *mud*, *cave*, and *dragon*. Write the adjectives on the board and ask the children to match them to the nouns. Choral practise: *long green* grass, *cold wet* water, *black sticky* mud, *big dark* cave, and *fierce fiery* dragon. Put the flashcards in place around the room saying 'Here's the grass', and so on.

2 Ask the children to tell you the noise that grass, water, and mud make as you go through them. Use their suggestions when you teach and act out the chorus (see step 5). Ask them:

How do you walk:
– when you are scared?
– if a dragon is chasing you?

3 Show the children the flashcards of the children going on the hunt. Ask them questions:

What are they going to do?
Why have they got sticks and a net?
How do they feel?
Is it easy to admit to being scared?

4 Tell them that these children say *We're not scared*. Ask the children to walk around as if they were scared and then pretending not to be scared.

5 Teach the first verse. Make sure that the children understand that they should listen and then repeat what you say using the same rhythm.

Teacher · ● · · ● · ·
We're going on a dragon hunt

Children · ● · · ● · ·
We're going on a dragon hunt

and so on.

6 Practise the first verse as the children stride out round the room, or on the spot if you don't have much space. If at all possible you should be joining in the action with the children .

7 Lead the children to the grass. Teach them the next part of the poem:

Teacher · ●
Oh no!

Children · ●
Oh no!

Teacher ● · · ●
Grass, long green grass

Children ● · · ●
Grass, long green grass

8 Teach the children the chorus, using appropriate actions as you do so:

Teacher · ● · ● ·
We can't go over it

Children · ● · ● ·
We can't go over it

Teacher We can't go under it
Children We can't go under it
Teacher We can't go round it
Children We can't go round it
Teacher We must go through it
Children We must go through it.
Teacher Swish, swish
Swish, swish, swish
Children Swish, swish
Swish, swish, swish

9 Teach the children verses 3, 4, and 5 in the same way.

10 Lead the children quickly from place to place as you teach them verse 6. When they get back home, ask them how they would feel if they had really escaped from a dragon. Ask them to show you with their bodies and faces.

11 Repeat the poem from the beginning, with a different group of actors if you are working with a large class. The children who are not acting can join in with the chorus.

FOLLOW-UP

One of the children can take your place as the leader, while the other children repeat.

COMMENTS

If you have a large class, you will need to divide them into actors and the chorus. Fifteen children as actors are probably the maximum possible.

2.8 A story chant

LEVEL	2, 3
AGE GROUP	**A, B (alternative version for age group C in variation)**
TIME	**20–30 minutes**
AIMS	**Language:** to practise listening for specific words or phrases. **Other:** to work together to act out a story.

DESCRIPTION

The children stand in a circle and do actions as the teacher chants or sings the story rhyme. There are two examples here: a traditional English story rhyme, and an invented rhyme of my own. It is not difficult to invent simple story rhymes that fit in with the topic you are working on in class.

MATERIALS

Flashcards or board pictures of a princess, a high tower, a wicked fairy, a wand, a forest, a prince, and an axe (see Worksheet 2.8).

PREPARATION

1 Learn the rhyme and practise it.
2 Make the flashcards.

IN CLASS

1 Tell the children you are going to tell them a story. Show them the flashcards or board pictures and teach them the words. Ask them what they think it will be about.
2 Tell the story and ask the children to put the cards in the order that they hear about them, or to number the board pictures.
3 Get the children to stand in a circle, and choose a princess, a wicked fairy, and a prince. Explain that they are going to act out the story (see story and actions box). Teach the actions one verse at a time, and then chant the story and do the actions right through.

FOLLOW-UP

With certain classes you may like to ask the children if they think the story could be told 'the other way round', with the princess rescuing the prince. This can lead to an interesting first-language discussion of the roles in stories and in real life. You can try acting it out the other way round too.

COMMENTS

Although the children are not asked to learn the words, you may find that after acting out the story several times they begin to join in with you.

VARIATION

A more modern story, which may appeal to older children, is given below. Older children with more English can try to invent a story of their own. They will need help in getting the rhythm of the verses right.

EXAMPLES   **The Princess song** (traditional)

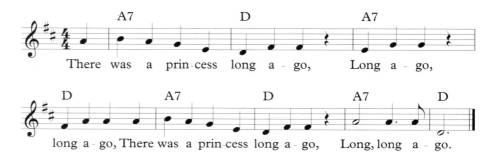

There was a prin-cess long a-go, Long a-go,
long a-go, There was a prin-cess long a-go, Long, long a - go.

Lyrics	*Actions*
There was a princess long ago Long ago, long ago There was a princess long ago Long, long ago.	*The children stand in a circle holding hands, the princess stands in the middle. The children move round slowly. The fairy and the prince stand outside the circle.*
And she lived in a high, high tower High, high tower, high, high tower And she lived in a high, high tower Long, long ago.	*The children raise their hands to make a high tower as they move round.*
A wicked fairy waved her wand Waved her wand, waved her wand A wicked fairy waved her wand Long, long ago.	*The fairy waves her wand, the children stop moving and the princess lies down and sleeps.*
The princess slept for a hundred years A hundred years, a hundred years The princess slept for a hundred years Long, long ago.	*Everyone lies or crouches down with their heads on their hands, sleeping.*
A great big forest grew around Grew around, grew around A great big forest grew around Long, long ago.	*The children get up slowly, stretching their arms up high, and waving them like trees in the wind.*
A handsome prince came riding by Riding by, riding by A handsome prince came riding by Long, long ago.	*The prince rides round the outside of the circle.*

He cut the trees down one
    by one
One by one, one by one
He cut the trees down one
    by one
Long, long ago.

The prince makes chopping movements with his hands and cuts the trees down.

He took the princess by
    the hand
By the hand, by the hand
He took the princess by
    the hand
Long, long ago.

The prince enters the circle and takes the princess by the hand. The children get up and the prince and princess join the circle.

So everybody's happy now
Happy now, happy now
So everybody's happy now
Happy, happy now.

The children skip round faster and faster.

There was a girl who had a cat (modern version)

Decide who is going to be:
- the girl
- the cat
- the aliens
- the spacecraft

Actions

There was a girl who had a cat
Had a cat, had a cat
There was a girl who had a cat
Long, long ago.

The children form a circle with the girl and cat and the friend in the middle. The children circle round slowly.

The aliens stole her cat away
Cat away, cat away
The aliens stole her cat away
Long, long ago.

The aliens break out of the circle, form a circle round the cat and carry it away. The other children stand still.

She built a spacecraft with her
    friend
With her friend, with her friend
She built a spacecraft with
    her friend
Long, long ago.

The girl and the friend build a spacecraft with the other children and get into it.

They chased the aliens to
    the moon
To the moon, to the moon
They chased the aliens to
    the moon
Long, long ago.

The spacecraft chases the aliens. When the aliens get to the moon they scatter, taking the cat with them. The girl and friend get out of their spacecraft.

There they found some
     magic dust
Magic dust, magic dust
There they found some
     magic dust
Long, long ago.

The girl and friend walk around and find the magic dust. The aliens move their arms menacingly.

They turned the aliens
     into stone
Into stone, into stone
They turned the aliens
     into stone
Long, long ago.

They sprinkle the dust over the aliens who 'freeze'.

They took the cat and went
     back home
Went back home, went
     back home
They took the cat and went
     back home
Long, long ago.

They rescue the cat, get back into the spacecraft, and fly home.

3 Making puppets and props

Puppets are a very versatile resource in the young learners' classroom. Children use language while making them, often respond to puppets more readily than to the teacher, and are usually enthusiastic about manipulating them. The process of making a puppet is a rewarding craft activity in itself and the end product, the puppet, plays a key role in a subsequent activity.

The way children respond to puppets is fascinating: they are willing to suspend belief, and react to the puppet as if it were real. This can be a useful way of stimulating learners to produce language: many teachers have a puppet that 'only speaks English', and use it effectively to encourage their children to speak in English throughout the lesson. In addition, puppets promote real communication tasks as children attempt to discover the names, ages, likes, and dislikes of puppets made by other learners. When children use a puppet as their mouthpiece, they often lose their reticence and hide behind it, participating in a way that they would not if they were asked to act out the part themselves. The language becomes one step removed.

In this chapter you will find instructions for making a variety of puppets. All of them are very simple and range from temporary ones, like 'faces on fists', to longer-lasting ones, like 'sock puppets'. You can use ready-made puppets, but if the children make them themselves they will have a sense of ownership when they use the puppets in drama activities. The song, dialogue, improvisation, or play will be more personal and memorable. Most of the puppets can be made in 10–15 minutes, so that you can then concentrate on using them to produce language.

There are also instructions for making very simple puppet theatres. The theatres are basic, and add an extra dramatic touch when the children show puppet activities to their classmates, because the main aim of these activities is not to produce something for the public, but rather to exploit the children's enjoyment of using puppets for language production.

In the last part of the chapter there are some instructions for making simple props, like hats and masks, which can be used when you do songs, role plays, and plays. They are all easy to make and don't require elaborate materials or a lot of time. However, they are valuable tools for helping children to 'get into' their role and become part of the 'play' world. Like the puppets, they provide protection for children who are shy about speaking. There are more ideas for making puppets in *Young Learners*.

3.1 Face on a finger

LEVEL	1, 2
AGE GROUP	A, B
TIME	5–10 minutes
DESCRIPTION	The children draw faces on their fingers. They can make hats or 'skirts' for them too.
AIMS	**Language:** following instructions. **Other:** preparing puppets for acting out; working on hand co-ordination.
MATERIALS	Washable felt-tip pens, strips of white and/or coloured paper if you want to make skirts, scissors, and fingers.
PREPARATION	Practise making a puppet on your finger.

IN CLASS

1 Tell the children they are going to make a puppet and that you are going to show them how. If you are using the puppets for a play, tell learners which characters they need.
2 Use the washable pens to draw a face halfway up your index finger.
3 Take a strip of paper and stick it into a circle that just fits the top of your finger. Cut and/or colour it to make hair or a hat. Put the paper on your finger.

4 Ask the children what they are going to need. Make sure everyone has the materials before they start.
5 Give the children 5–10 minutes to make their puppets.

VARIATION   The children draw puppets on their partner's finger.

3.2   Face on a fist

LEVEL	**1, 2**
AGE GROUP	**A, B**
TIME	**5–10 minutes**
AIMS	**Language:** following instructions. **Other:** to make puppets.
DESCRIPTION	The children draw faces on their fists (see picture). They can raise and lower their thumb to make the puppet speak.
MATERIALS	Washable felt-tip pens and hands.
PREPARATION	Practise drawing the puppet on your fist and making it talk (see illustration).

IN CLASS

1 If you are going to use the puppets for a play, tell the children who the characters are.
2 Tell them to close their fists and draw on the eyes, lips, and hair.
3 Practise raising and lowering your thumb to show them how to make the puppet speak.
4 Put the children into pairs and get them to draw the puppets onto each other's fists.

3.3   Finger tube puppet

LEVEL	**2, 3**
AGE GROUP	**A, B**
TIME	**15 minutes**
AIMS	**Language:** giving and receiving instructions; body vocabulary. **Other:** to encourage creativity and make puppets for use in class on such activities as 2.4, 'Two tall daddies'.
DESCRIPTION	The children make a tube of paper to fit over their finger. They draw a face and costume on the paper. These puppets have the advantage

of being slightly longer-lasting and can be more elaborate than simply painting a face onto a finger. You can use these puppets with the rhyme, 2.4, 'Two tall daddies'.

MATERIALS

Pieces of white and/or coloured paper, and coloured pens or felt tips.

PREPARATION

Prepare a puppet yourself to show the children.

IN CLASS

1 Show the children your puppet and tell them they are going to make a similar one.

2 Cut out a rectangle of paper. It needs to be about the height of the children's fingers and long enough to wrap twice round. This double wrap gives the puppet a little more strength.

3 Draw the features of the puppet (see diagram). Add hair, ears, buttons, and so on, using scraps of coloured paper or coloured pens. As you do so, give simple instructions like *draw the ears, stick on the hair.*

4 Ask the children what materials they need, and tell them to make sure they have everything before they start.

5 Go through the instructions again.

6 Tell them to take it in turns to instruct each other on how to make the puppet. As they work, go around the class, commenting and helping if necessary.

7 The children will need about 15 minutes to make a simple puppet. They could, of course, take much longer if they want to make a more elaborate one.

3.4 Sponge puppet

LEVEL
All

AGE GROUP
A, B

TIME
20 minutes

AIMS
Language: following instructions.
Other: working on co-operation and helping each other.

DESCRIPTION
The children make a puppet using a bath sponge as a base. You can use these puppets in 4.5, 'Animating the textbook'.

MATERIALS
A cheap oval bath sponge per child, glue, and scraps of paper, card, or felt.

PREPARATION
Make a puppet yourself to show the children.

IN CLASS
1 Have all the materials you need, nearby. Show the sponge and tell them to watch you as you make the puppet. Talk through the process as you show them how to make it.
2 Cut holes in the back of the sponge for your fingers and thumb.
3 Cut out eyes, ears, hair, teeth, and so on. Stick them on the sponge.

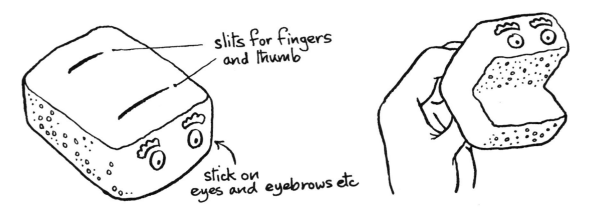

4 Put your fingers in the holes and use them to make the sponge talk.
5 Get the children to collect the material they need before they start.
6 Tell them to make their puppets in pairs, helping each other and giving advice.
7 Go around the class encouraging and commenting as they make their puppets.

3.5 Origami puppet

LEVEL	**All**
AGE GROUP	**B, C**
TIME	**15 minutes to make the basic form and 15 minutes to decorate it.**
AIMS	**Language:** following spoken instructions. **Other:** develop manual dexterity, create a character through physical features.
MATERIALS	A piece of A4-size paper, blank on at least one side; crayons or felt tips, coloured paper, scissors, glue.
DESCRIPTION	The children follow spoken instructions and make an origami puppet from a piece of A4 paper. There is a suggestion for using these puppets in 4.8, 'Puppet conversations'.

PREPARATION

1 Make the puppet base yourself. Make sure that you can make it 'in the air' while demonstrating the folds to your children.
2 Practise explaining how to make the puppet to a colleague if you can. This will help you discover possible problems.
3 Make and decorate a puppet to show to the children.

IN CLASS

1 Show the children your puppet and tell them they are going to make one too.
2 Give out the paper.
3 Give instructions on making the puppet like this:

Fold the paper in half like this.

Now fold it in half again.

Now fold it this way.

Now make a zigzag like this.

Find these little pockets. Put your fingers in them and make your puppet talk.

4 Get the children to try following the above instructions to make the puppet in pairs first, and then they can make their own.

5 When they have finished making the puppet, show the children how to make the puppet's face. The children can cut out paper features and stick them on.

3.6 Sock puppet

LEVEL	**All**
AGE GROUP	**B, C**
TIME	**40 minutes**
AIMS	**Language:** to follow instructions. **Other:** to prepare the puppet for use in a story.
DESCRIPTION	The children make a puppet using a sock as a base. When you put your four fingers in the toe of the sock and the palm of your hand or your thumb in the heel, you make a mouth that opens and closes. Although they take longer to make, they are stronger and longer lasting than the ones described previously. They are also suitable to use as your own puppet who 'only speaks English'. There is a suggestion for using these puppets in 4.1, 'Yes and no puppets'.
MATERIALS	An old sock per child, coloured wool, table tennis balls or balls of cotton wool for eyes (optional), scraps of coloured card or felt, coloured pens or crayons.

PREPARATION

1 Tell the children at least a week before the lesson that they need to bring an old sock to school. The children's own socks will probably be too small; an older child's or an adult sock is better.

2 Make several puppets, each at a different stage of completion. These are useful when demonstrating how to make the puppet.

IN CLASS

1 Show the children your finished puppet and explain that they are going to make one themselves.

2 Show the children all the materials they will need, naming them and writing a list on the board. Ask them to find the material they are going to use.

3 Show them the different stages one at a time. Describe what they have to do, demonstrating at the same time. Wait until all the children have finished one stage before you demonstrate the next. Make the puppet like this:

a Put your hand in the sock and mark where the hair will go. Glue or sew short pieces of wool in place.

b Cut out an oval piece of card which fits the inside of the mouth. Colour it red and then glue it in place. You can stick on teeth and a tongue too: these are very useful for making a snake or 'Dracula'.

c Make eyes out of the table tennis balls, cotton wool balls or circles of card by drawing black dots in the middle. Glue them in place.

VARIATION

You can make a simple puppet with arms, using a sock and a glove. Make holes in the sock for the 'arms' and wear the glove 'inside' the sock.

3.7 Shadow puppet

LEVEL

All

AGE GROUP

All

TIME

10 minutes upwards (depending on the complexity of the puppet)

AIMS

Language: following instructions.
Other: to stimulate creativity and use puppets to reinforce and act out a play activity like the ones in Chapter 5.

DESCRIPTION

The children cut out a face or figure with a clear silhouette. They mount it on their fingers or a stick, and use the puppets with a shadow puppet theatre (see 3.9, variation 5, 'A shadow puppet theatre'). There is an activity for using shadow puppets in 4.4, 'Telling a story with shadow puppets'.

| **MATERIALS** | Pencils, photocopiable card or card and paper, scissors, sticky tape, and thin sticks; photocopies or drawings of the characters for your story, for example, 'The Little Red Hen' (see 4.4 for the story and Worksheet 3.7 for the figures). |

PREPARATION

1 Decide on the story or situation you are going to use the puppets in.

2 Photocopy the figures on the worksheet, or design your own. If possible, copy the figures on to thin card (this saves sticking the paper figures on to card later).

3 Make the puppets yourself.

4 Make a simple shadow puppet theatre (see 3.9, 'A shadow puppet theatre').

IN CLASS

1 Set up the theatre and show the children the puppets and how they work. Move them around behind the screen, perhaps using them to tell the children a short story.

2 Give out the photocopies and tell the children they are going to make a puppet.

3 Cut out the figures and fix them to the stick. If the copies are on paper, stick them on to card first.

VARIATION 1

Stick a loop of card to the figures and put your finger or thumb through it instead of using a stick.

VARIATION 2

If you want coloured figures, cut out parts of the figure and stick coloured cellophane over the space. The light will shine through the cellophane to make a coloured shadow.

VARIATION 3

You can make jointed figures using paper fasteners and sticking one stick to each moving part, for example, the body and an arm (see 3.8, 'Stick puppets').

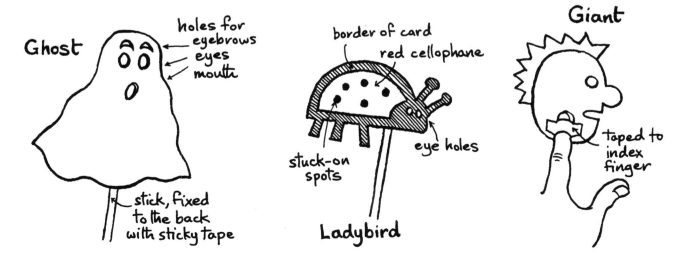

3.8   Stick puppet

LEVEL	**All**
AGE GROUP	**All**
TIME	**20 minutes**
AIMS	**Language:** following instructions. **Other:** to make a puppet for use in such activities as 4.3, 'Big Blue Fish and Small Red Fish'.
DESCRIPTION	The children cut out figures like the ones in Worksheet 4.3 for 'Big Blue Fish and Small Red Fish'. They colour them.
MATERIALS	Photocopies or drawings of the figures you want to use. Two sticks for each puppet, coloured pencils, scissors, card, glue, a split pin for each puppet, sticky tape.

PREPARATION

1 Choose the story you want to use the puppets in.
2 Make a puppet.
3 Make a theatre (see next section).

IN CLASS

1 Draw or photocopy the outline of the character you want to use on to thin card.
2 Colour it and draw eyes, a mouth, and so on on to the figure.
3 If you want the puppet to have a moving part, for example, an arm, or a fin for the fish puppets in 4.3, attach the fin to the figure with a split pin.
4 Attach one thin stick on to the back of the puppet and one on to the fin. Move the fin using the stick.

3.9   Simple puppet theatres

LEVEL	**All**
AGE GROUP	**All**
TIME	**5–15 minutes**
AIMS	**Language:** to follow instructions **Other:** to make a theatre for use with puppets in this chapter and for plays in Chapter 5.

IN CLASS

Unless you are going to use puppets a great deal in class, or are going to put on a puppet show for parents and friends, it is not necessary to have an elaborate theatre. Here are some simple ideas that you can use in most classrooms:

VARIATION 1

Put two or three tables or chairs together in a line and get the children to crouch behind them. You can pin a sheet or a length of paper across the front of the desks to hide the puppeteers.

VARIATION 2

Pin an old sheet across the classroom door, high enough for the children to hide behind. The puppeteers go into the passage while the audience stays in the classroom.

VARIATION 3

You (and the children) can make a more permanent puppet booth with a box for domestic appliances like a washing machine or dishwasher. Cut a hole in the back for the puppeteers to go in and out of, and a hole in the front for the puppets. Paint the box with poster paints.

VARIATION 4

Make a mini theatre for small stick puppets out of a grocery box. Cut holes in the front and sides and paint the box. You can make backdrops painted with suitable backgrounds to fit the back of the box.

VARIATION 5

A shadow puppet theatre

Make a shadow theatre using a large cardboard box. Cut out one of the biggest sides, cut a hole in it and make a screen by sticking white (or coloured) crêpe paper over the hole. Attach the screen to the back of a chair with wide sticky tape. Set up a lamp behind the screen.

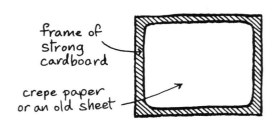

3.10 Hat base

LEVEL	**All**
AGE GROUP	**B, C**
TIME	**15 minutes folding and 15 minutes decorating.**
AIMS	**Language:** following instructions, parts of the body. **Other:** develop precision in paper folding skills.
DESCRIPTION	The children fold stiff paper to make a hat which they can then decorate. You can use these hats in the story chant (see 2.8).
MATERIALS	A square of paper 50–60 cm square. The length of the side should be the same as the circumference of the child's head. You can use newspaper, though if you want a stronger hat, it is best to use parcel wrapping paper, which can now often be bought in various colours.

PREPARATION

1 Make a hat yourself.
2 Unfold your hat and make it again: practise giving instructions as you fold.
3 Practise giving instructions to a colleague if you can.
4 If possible, teach three or four children from your class how to make the hat before you teach the whole class. When the children have mastered it, they will be able to act as your helpers in class. You may like to ask them to keep the activity a secret.

IN CLASS

1 Show the children a square of paper and ask them to guess what you are going to make.
2 Make the hat in front of the children, talking through each step.

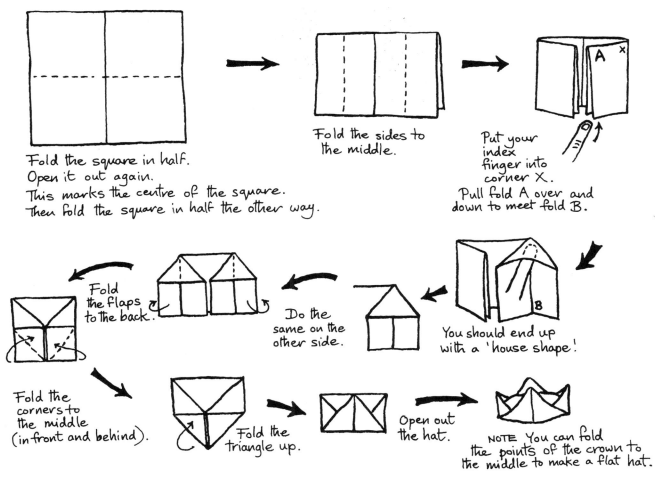

Fold the square in half.
Open it out again.
This marks the centre of the square.
Then fold the square in half the other way.

Fold the sides to the middle.

Put your index finger into corner X.
Pull fold A over and down to meet fold B.

You should end up with a 'house shape'!

Do the same on the other side.

Fold the flaps to the back.

Fold the corners to the middle (in front and behind).

Fold the triangle up.

Open out the hat.

NOTE You can fold the points of the crown to the middle to make a flat hat.

3 Tell the children to clear their desks and give out the pieces of paper. If you have got some helpers (see Preparation) ask them to be ready to help if necessary.

4 Demonstrate how to make the hat again, step by step. Don't move on to the next step until all the children are ready.

5 When the base is finished, the children can decorate them as necessary.

For an idea for making an all-purpose hat see *Very Young Learners*, Further Reading.

3.11 Headband

LEVEL	**All**
AGE GROUP	**All**
TIME	**15 minutes**
AIMS	**Language:** following instructions. **Other:** developing craft skills.

DESCRIPTION

The children make a headband out of card and decorate it as appropriate. For example, add:

- ears to make animals;
- antennae to make insects or space monsters;
- feathers to make Indians;
- leaves, flowers, and fruit to make trees and bushes;
- numbers, letters, shapes to use the bands in team games.

You can use these headbands in songs and plays where you only need a simple indication of character.

MATERIALS

Card, sticky tape, scissors, coloured pens, glue.

PREPARATION

1 Make a headband yourself.

2 Cut strips of card about 7 cm wide and long enough to fit the children's heads and add a little more. This will make an overlap for sticking.

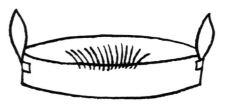

IN CLASS

1 Show the children how to make the headband, talking the steps through as you go.

2 Tell the children to find the materials they need before you start.

3 Cut a strip of card long enough to go round your head and overlap slightly.

4 Decorate it and then stick the ends together to the right size.

5 Add appropriate decoration.

6 Give out the bands for the children to decorate.

7 Stick the bands together yourself as the children finish.

8 The children can stick the decoration on with sticky tape.

3.12   A half mask

LEVEL

All

AGE GROUP

All

TIME

20–25 minutes

AIMS

Language: following instructions.
Other: developing craft skills.

DESCRIPTION

The children use the mask base (see Worksheet 3.12) to make a mask.

MATERIALS

Enough copies of the mask base, on card if possible; hat elastic (about 30 cm for each child); colours, scissors, glue, card (if you can not make copies on card).

PREPARATION

1 Make a mask for a character yourself. Add features, fur, or eyebrows to the upper outline, but the lower outline should be left as it is, so that it fits over your nose.
2 Make enough copies of the mask base, on card if possible.
3 Cut the elastic into 30 cm lengths.

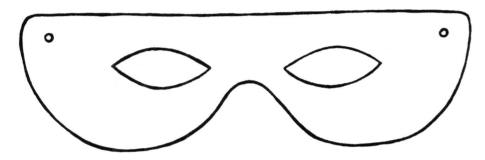

IN CLASS

1 Show the children the mask you have made. Tell them to make one. Explain that they can adapt the base to make any animal or character they want to: it is only a guide.
2 Ask the children to clear their desks and find the material they need.
3 Give out the mask bases. Go around the class, commenting and encouraging the children as they work.
4 As the children finish, put the elastic in their masks. Make a hole where marked. Then put the elastic through the hole and tie it round. Older children may be able to do it themselves.

3.13 Mask on a stick

LEVEL

All

AGE GROUP

All

TIME

20–25 minutes

AIMS

Language: following instructions.
Other: developing craft skills.

DESCRIPTION

The children decorate a paper plate or cardboard circle and attach it to a stick to make a hand-held mask.

MATERIALS

Paper plates or circles of card for each child; a stick for each child; strong tape, colours, glue, scissors.

PREPARATION

Make a mask yourself.

IN CLASS

1 Show the children your mask.

2 Ask the children what they need and make a list on the board.

3 Tell the children to make sure they have everything to make the mask before they start.

4 If you are going to use the masks in a play, make sure each child knows which mask to make.

Making the mask

5 Draw circles on the plate for the eyes and cut them out.

6 Add a nose and mouth.

7 Decorate the mask, according to the character.

8 Stick a thin stick on the back using strong tape.

9 As the children are working, walk around the class commenting and helping where necessary.

4 Using puppets

Puppets have many other uses in addition to the ones outlined in the previous chapter. Puppets can be used with songs, chants, dialogues, improvisations, and plays like the ones in Chapter 5. They encourage children to use their imaginations freely in acting out and using language, even in a confined space. Puppets allow you to make elaborate characters, even ghosts, monsters, dinosaurs, and so on, which are difficult to achieve on stage. They can be used with stories you tell the children and ones they invent themselves.

Using puppets calls for some of the same skills as acting—using your voice, co-operation between puppeteers, and memorization, but it also uses different ones. Puppeteers need to learn how to manipulate the puppets, open their mouths in time, hold the puppets still, turn and move them appropriately, as well as enter and exit with care. While these skills are vital in a professional puppeteer, the children only need to control the puppets sufficiently to make the play or sketch interesting and understandable to an audience of their peers. If you are going to ask the children to use puppets regularly, it is worthwhile focusing on these skills in the feedback sessions, and helping the children towards an awareness of them.

Puppets add variety, and sometimes a touch of magic, to the activities the children do in their language class. You may find that children who are not always co-operative, or who do not show a great deal of interest in class, will respond very positively to puppets. They combine the visual, aural, and kinaesthetic (physical) in a way that is hard to resist.

4.1 *Yes* and *no* puppets

LEVEL	**All**
AGE GROUP	**A, B**
TIME	**20 minutes**
AIMS	**Language:** to present and practise questions, affirmatives, and negatives of a given structure (in this example *like*). **Other:** to practise working with puppets in pairs.
DESCRIPTION	The teacher uses a red and a green sock puppet (see 3.6, 'Sock puppet') to present the questions, affirmative, and negative of a structure, for example: *Have you got …? Yes, I have. No, I haven't.* The children can make their own puppets to practise with.

MATERIALS

Two sock (or other) puppets in red and green (or other contrasting colours); items to practise with, for example, fruit for *I like*, toys for *I've got*, different kinds of balls/rackets for *I'm going to*, and so on.

PREPARATION

1 Make the puppets (see 3.6, 'Sock puppet').

2 Practise the presentation, especially if you are not used to using puppets.

IN CLASS

In this example the structure is *Have you got ...? Yes, I have. No, I haven't.* You can adapt the procedure for other structures as necessary.

1 Show the children the puppets. If it is the first time you have used them, tell the children their names, for example: Yolanda Yes (the green puppet) and Nicky No (the red puppet). Explain that Yolanda Yes always says *yes*, and Nicky No always says *no*.

2 Get the puppet to ask the children their names and a yes/no question (for example, *Are you nine?*). If possible get the children to ask the puppets questions, making Yolanda answer *yes* and Nicky answer *no*.

3 Show the children the toys you have brought in. Alternatively, you can use objects from a pencil case. Check they know the names of the toys or objects.

4 Set the situation by telling the children that Yolanda and Nicky have a toy shop. Yolanda wants to sell lots of things, but Nicky wants to keep them for himself.

Teacher	Good morning, Yolanda. Good morning, Nicky.
Yolanda	Good morning.
Nicky	Good morning.
Yolanda	Can I help you?
Teacher	Well, I want a car. Have you got a car?
Yolanda	Yes, we have (*starts to give teacher the car*).
Nicky	No, we haven't (*takes it away and hides it*).
Teacher	Oh well, have you got a robot?
Yolanda	Yes, we have (*starts to give teacher the robot*).
Nicky	No, we haven't (*takes it away and hides it*).

Continue until you think the children are ready to try using the puppets themselves.

5 Teach the children the question, and then let them take your role and ask the puppets.

6 Check the children can say the answers, and ask for three volunteers to try the conversation.

FOLLOW-UP

The children make their own puppets and practise the conversation in threes.

4.2   Guessing games

LEVEL	**All**
AGE GROUP	**B, C**
TIME	**10–15 minutes**
AIMS	**Language:** to revise and recycle vocabulary, to ask *yes/no* questions. **Other:** to encourage children to solve problems by making and testing hypotheses.

DESCRIPTION

The teacher uses a puppet (see Chapter 3) to set a problem for the children to solve. For example, the puppet tells the children what food it likes and doesn't like. This may be according to the type of food (for example, it may like white food but not coloured food) or spelling (for example, it may like food spelt with a double letter and not food without a double letter). The children ask the puppet questions to solve the problem.

MATERIALS

A puppet; fruit and vegetables or flashcards of them.

IN CLASS

1 Show the children the fruit and vegetables and check they can name them.

2 Ask them which fruits and vegetables they like and dislike. Check they can ask the question: *Do you like …?*

3 Explain that the puppet is going to tell them what she likes and dislikes and that they have to guess why.

4 Get the puppet to say *I like carrots, I don't like apples, I like potatoes, I don't like oranges*. Encourage the children to think of what the puppet's likes and dislikes have in common (in this case, it likes vegetables but not fruit).

5 Get them to discuss their ideas in pairs and then think of some questions to ask the puppet to see if they are right.

6 Let the children ask their questions.

   If the children are getting frustrated, help them by making a list of the puppets' likes and dislikes on the board. Ask key questions to guide them to the answer.

VARIATION

This could be done with other topics, for example, sports. Get the puppet to say *I can't play football, I can swim, I can't play tennis, I can ski* (the puppet can't do sports that use a ball).

COMMENTS

Andrew Wright's *1000+ Pictures for Teachers to Copy* has easy pictures of people playing different sports.

4.3 Telling a story with stick puppets: 'Big Blue Fish and Small Red Fish'

LEVEL	1, 2
AGE GROUP	A, B
TIME	**20 minutes + 20 minutes**
AIMS	**Language:** prepositions of place, *Where are you?*, and *Help!*; re-writing a story following a model (older children). **Other:** co-operating in re-telling a story.
MATERIALS	Stick puppets of Big Blue Fish and Small Red Fish (see Chapter 3); flashcards with a flap on them (seaweed, shells, rocks, old boot, picnic basket; see Worksheet 4.3); blu-tack; the story (later in this section).
DESCRIPTION	The teacher uses stick puppets (see 3.8, 'Stick puppets') to tell the children a story. The children can then make the puppets themselves and use them to act out the same story or use it as a model to write and act out their own version of it.
PREPARATION	1 Make the puppets.
	2 Make the flashcards.
	3 Practise telling the story with the puppets.
IN CLASS	1 Show the children the fish puppets and tell them their names.
	2 Draw a wavy blue line high on the board to represent the sea, and draw some sand at the bottom of the board. Stick the flashcards on to the board. See illustration.

3 Use the puppets to tell the story; there are suggested actions with the story on the next page to help you.

Teach the children the key phrases in the story, and tell it again. This time you can divide the class into two halves; one half can say the lines of Big Blue Fish and the other the lines of Small Red Fish.

5 Ask two children to come to the board and move the puppets as the class says the dialogue.

FOLLOW-UP

The children make their own puppets and props and use them to practise the story.

STORY OUTLINE

BIG BLUE FISH AND SMALL RED FISH

Story	Actions
This is Big Blue Fish. She was very, very big.	*Show the children the Big Blue Fish (BBF) puppet.*
And this is Small Red Fish. She was very, very small.	*Show the Small Red Fish (SRF) puppet.*
They lived in the deep blue sea.	*Make the fish swim in the sea.*
Small Red Fish was frightened of Big Blue Fish.	*Make SRF tremble.*
One day Big Blue Fish said in a loud voice, 'I'm hungry. I'm very, very hungry! Where are you, Small Red Fish?'	*Hold BBF up as you talk.*
'Oh, help! Help! Help!' said Small Red Fish. 'Where can I hide?'	*Move SRF backwards and forwards looking for somewhere to hide.*
And Small Red Fish hid under a shell.	*Hide SRF under the shell.*
But Big Blue Fish could see her tail. 'There you are!' she said in a loud voice.	*Move BBF towards the shell.*
But Small Red Fish just escaped in time. 'I'm hungry' said Big Blue Fish. 'Where are you, Small Red Fish?'	*Make SRF escape and hide behind the seaweed.*
'Oh, help! help! help!' said Small Red Fish. 'Where can I hide?'	*Move SRF backwards and forwards looking for somewhere to hide.*
And she hid behind a rock.	*Hide SRF behind a rock.*
But Big Blue Fish could see her tail. 'There you are!' she said in a loud voice.	*Move BBF towards the rock.*

But Small Red Fish just escaped in time.	*SRF escapes and hides behind the seaweed.*
'I'm hungry' said Big Blue Fish. 'Where are you, Small Red Fish?'	
'Oh, help!, help! help!' said Small Red Fish. 'Where can I hide?'	*Move SRF backwards and forwards looking for somewhere to hide.*
And she hid in a boot.	*Hide SRF in the boot.*
But Big Red Fish could see her tail. 'There you are' she said. And this time Small Red Fish couldn't escape.	*Move BRF towards the boot.*
'Please don't eat me' said Small Red Fish.	*Make SRF tremble.*
'Eat you!' said Big Blue Fish laughing, 'Eat you! I'm hungry. You're very, very small.'	*Hold BBF up and laugh.*
'Oh' said Small Red Fish and she came out of the boot.	*Make SRF come out of the boot.*
'I've got a picnic' said Big Blue Fish. 'Come and have a picnic with me!'	*Move BBF to the picnic basket.*
So Big Blue Fish and Small Red Fish had a picnic together, and from that day they were good friends.	*Move SRF to the picnic basket.* *Stick them both to the board with blu-tack.*

VARIATION

This story also works well with shadow puppets. The fish can be made by sticking red and blue cellophane on to the fish outlines. The shell, rock, and boot are made by mounting cut outs on to sticks.

4.4 Telling a story with shadow puppets: 'The Little Red Hen'

LEVEL

All

AGE GROUP

All

TIME

40 minutes

AIMS

Language: to listen attentively to the information in a story so that you are able to re-tell it.

Other: to co-ordinate words and movement and collaborate with others to produce a piece of work.

DESCRIPTION

The teacher tells a story using shadow puppets (see 3.7, 'Shadow puppets'). The children then make puppets of their own and re-tell the story. Older children can write a parallel story and make puppets for it.

MATERIALS

Card, cellophane, and sticks to make the shadow; a shadow puppet theatre (see 3.9, 'A shadow puppet theatre', variation 5).

PREPARATION

1 Decide on the story you are going to tell. There is a story skeleton of 'The Little Red Hen' below.

2 Make the shadow puppets. There are templates for the characters in 'The Little Red Hen' on Worksheet 4.4.

3 Practise telling the story as you manipulate the puppets.

IN CLASS

1 Show the children the puppets. Tell them their names.

2 Mix up the words from step 4 and teach them to the children. Ask them to put them in a logical order.

3 Use the puppets to tell the story.

4 Write the appropriate verb next to each noun:

grains of wheat	*found*
	plant
wheat	*cut*
wheat sheaf	*take the wheat sheaf to the mill*
flour	*take the flour to the baker*
bread	*eat*

5 Ask the children if they can remember the question the Little Red Hen asked. (*Will/Can/Could you help me …?*) Practise the questions for each part of the story.

6 Ask the children if they can remember what the animals replied. (*I'm too busy, tired, hot.*) Practise the answers for each part of the story.

7 Ask the children what the animals said when they offered to help eat the bread. (*Shall I help you eat the bread?*) Practise the question.

8 Ask for four volunteers to manipulate the puppets while you and the class tell the story again. You may like to divide the class into four groups, giving each group a part.

FOLLOW-UP 1

Ask the children if they think the animals acted as good friends to the Little Red Hen. *Was she right not to share the bread? What else could she have done? What are the characteristics of a good friend?*

FOLLOW-UP 2

In another class, get the children to make the puppets and use them to act out the story themselves.

FOLLOW-UP 3

Older children can take the basic story and change and personalize it. They can change the characters and the setting, which will naturally lead to changing the dialogue.

STORY OUTLINE

THE LITTLE RED HEN

The Little Red Hen lived on a farm with the Cat, the Pig, and the Mouse.

One day she found some grains of wheat.

'Will you help me plant the wheat?' she asked the Cat.

'Oh, no,' said the Cat, 'I'm too tired.'

'Can you help me plant the wheat?' she asked the Pig.

'Oh, no,' said the Pig, 'I'm too hot.'

'Could you help me plant the wheat?' she asked the Rat.

'Oh, no,' said the Rat, 'I'm too busy.'

'Well,' said the Little Red Hen, 'then I think I'll plant it myself.'

The seeds grew into wheat, and soon it was time to cut it.

'Will you help me cut the wheat?' she asked the Cat. [*and so on*]

Then the Little Red Hen had to take the wheat sheaf to the miller. It was quite heavy.

'Will you help me take the wheat sheaf to the mill?' she asked the Cat. [*and so on*]

Then she had to take the flour to the baker.

'Will you help me take the flour to the baker?' she asked the Cat. [*and so on*]

Then she took the beautiful loaf of bread to the farm.

'Shall I help you eat the bread?' asked the Cat.

'Shall I help you eat the bread?' asked the Pig.

'Shall I help you eat the bread?' asked the Rat.

'No, thank you,' said the Little Red Hen, 'I'm very hungry, and I think I'll eat it all myself!'

COMMENTS

According to the level of the children, you may like to limit the Hen's request for help to only one simple question form, for example, *Please help me …*, or make it more difficult by including *Will you …*, and others.

4.5 Animating the textbook

LEVEL

All

AGE GROUP

All

TIME

30 minutes

AIMS

Language: speaking, revision, and recycling of language from previous units.

Other: to bring the text alive, to stimulate memory, and to encourage children to improvise.

DESCRIPTION

The children use puppets to animate a text from their coursebook (see 3.8, 'Stick puppets', for the instructions for making stick puppets).

MATERIALS

A puppet for each child (these can be made in a previous lesson).

PREPARATION

1 Choose a text you have worked on and want to animate. It can be a dialogue or a story which contains dialogue. There should be at least two speaking parts and not more than five.

2 Get the children to make the puppets in a previous lesson. Each child needs to make one of the characters. If you are using a story with characters that appear at intervals throughout the book, and are planning to activate the stories on a regular basis, it is a good idea to make one of the more long-lasting puppets, for example, the sponge puppets, stick puppets, or sock puppets.

IN CLASS

1 Show the children the text and ask them if they can remember what happened.

2 Ask them if they can remember what any of the characters said. Write what they remember on the board.

3 Write up the rest of the dialogue on the board, out of order. Ask the children which character says what, and then ask them to order the dialogue. They can do this as a class, in pairs, or in groups.

4 Divide the children into groups, making sure that each group has one puppet for each character. Ask them to practise the dialogue. They should practise it three times: the first time looking at the board or their book, the second time 'half looking', and the third time they should try and remember (or improvise) the text.

5 Ask them to get out their puppets. The children practise saying the dialogue using their puppets. Remind them that the puppets should look at each other when they speak, and should not move too much.

6 Ask some of the groups to show the rest of the class their work.

7 If you are going to use puppets regularly, it is worth giving some feedback. For example, you can ask the children what advice they would give to another group doing the same activity. Make a poster of their suggestions and use it to remind the children the next time they work with puppets.

FOLLOW-UP

The children can use the text as a basis and adapt and change it as they like. They can change the words, the setting, and the characters.

VARIATION

Use a scene from a video (for example, *Wizadora*) to act out.

4.6   From situation to dialogue

LEVEL	2, 3
AGE GROUP	C
TIME	**45 minutes**

AIMS

Language: to activate the children's language resource.
Other: to stimulate the children's imagination and to encourage them to build a story and its dialogue together.

DESCRIPTION

The teacher sets a context through a board picture or description. The children invent a dialogue for the situation with help from the teacher or in small groups. Then they use the puppets to act it out.

MATERIALS

Materials necessary to make the puppets (see Chapter 3); flashcards or poster to set up the situation.

PREPARATION

1 Decide on the situation, how you are going to present it (through flashcards, a poster, realia, a board picture), and how many characters there are. There are some suggestions for situations in the box on page 77.
2 Decide what kind of puppet you want the children to make and make one yourself for each character.

IN CLASS

1 Set up the situation using board pictures, flashcards, and so on to help you. Ask the children what each of the characters would say. Accept their suggestions and use them to build up the beginning of the dialogue on the board.
2 Encourage them to continue the story if appropriate, asking 'What happened next?'
3 When you and the class are satisfied with the dialogue ask the children to make puppets for the characters and to use them to act out the dialogue, following the steps in activity 4.5, 'Animating the textbook'.

VARIATION 1

Use a cartoon strip with pictures that clearly tell the story. The children invent the words and then use puppets to act them out.

VARIATION 2

If the children are used to building dialogues you can put them in small groups and ask each group to work on its own text.

COMMENTS

As you will see from the situations below, you can use this activity to stimulate the children to solve problems, or encourage them to reflect on moral dilemmas.

> **Real or possible situations**
>
> Two children arriving late to class.
> A child about to cross the road when a car is coming.
> Three children and two lollipops.
> Two children locked into a park.
> Two children with enough money to buy one ice cream/sandwich/snack/cinema ticket, and so on.
>
> **Imaginary situations**
>
> Two children looking into a black hole in which they can see two yellow eyes.
> Two children and an alien or a monster.
> Two children needing to cross a river without a bridge.
> Two children find a large amount of money in the street.

4.7 At the doctor's

LEVEL	2, 3
AGE GROUP	B, C
TIME	**10–15 minutes to make the puppet; 15–20 minutes to prepare the improvisation; 10–15 minutes to do the improvisation and feedback. These three stages can be done in one or separate lessons.**
AIMS	**Language:** to encourage fluency in a given situation and to practise the language of illnesses and doctor's visits. **Other:** to stimulate the children's creativity.
DESCRIPTION	The children use puppets to act out a common situation, in this example a visit to the doctor's.
MATERIALS	Those needed to make the puppets (see Chapter 3); copies of role cards like those in 5.15, 'Make your own role card'.
PREPARATION	Make several role cards like the personal file card in 5.15, 'Make your own role card'. Make half of them for doctors (include name, where they work, and what kind of doctor they are) and half of them for patients (include things like the patient's problem and how they feel).
IN CLASS	**Preparing the character** 1 The children make either a 'patient' puppet or a 'doctor' puppet. The patient puppet may have something obviously wrong—a cut, spots—or they may have an ill expression. As the children are making the puppets, go round the class asking 'What's the matter?' and commenting on the children's work.

2 When they are finished, get the children to show the patient puppets to the rest of the class and say what is wrong with them.

3 Give each child a character sheet to complete for their puppet. This will help them invent a personality for their puppet, as well as make them think about concrete details such as name, age, and problem.

Preparing the dialogue

4 When they have finished the character sheet, brainstorm some useful expressions with the class and write them on the board. For example:

Good morning/afternoon … .
What's the matter?
Let me see!
How long have you had … ?
When did you … ?
Take this (twice a day).
Go home and rest.
I don't feel well.
I've got a terrible … .
My stomach hurts.
Ouch!
Thank you very much.

5 Use a patient and a doctor puppet to improvise a dialogue showing the children what you would like them to do.

6 Put the children into pairs and get them to work out a dialogue together using the character sheets and the phrases on the board to help them. They can write it down if they need to, though it is best to encourage them to write only key words which help them remember what they want to say.

7 Get the children to practise their dialogue with their puppets.

Acting out

8 If possible, arrange the desks in the classroom to represent a doctor's surgery, with two chairs facing each other at each desk. Ask the children to sit the doctor puppets behind the desks and line up the patient puppets at the front of the class. Act as a receptionist, asking the puppets their names, and showing them into the different doctors' surgeries. Once in the surgery, the puppets should play out the scene. Some of the language will be as they have prepared it, but they will need to improvise as well.

9 While the children are working on the improvisation, listen in and watch their work in order to give feedback on the performances.

FOLLOW-UP

When they have finished, ask them how they felt they did and comment on their work. You may like to ask them to think about how they could have improved their performances and use their comments next time you do an improvisation.

| VARIATION | This activity can be done in any situation where the language is fairly predictable, for example: in a shop, buying travel tickets, at customs, at a restaurant, at a hotel, talking to Father Christmas, or interviews with real or imaginary beings. |

4.8 Puppet conversations

| LEVEL | 2,3 |

| AGE GROUP | **All** |

| TIME | **20 minutes + 20 minutes** |

| AIMS | **Language:** to practise asking and giving personal information. **Other:** to create a character and to practise speaking to a puppet and making a puppet speak. |

| DESCRIPTION | The children make an animal using one of the puppet bases given in Chapter 3, and then invent a personal file for it. Then they talk to other puppets and discover as much information as they can about them. |

| MATERIALS | Any of the puppet bases. |

| PREPARATION | 1 Prepare an animal puppet yourself and invent its personal file. |
| | 2 Photocopy or prepare a personal file card for each child (see photocopiable file card below). |

Personal file card

Name _____

Country _____

Favourite food _____

Colour _____

What they can do _____

Photocopiable © Oxford University Press

IN CLASS	1 Show the class your puppet and get them to ask it some questions.
	2 Put the children in pairs and tell them that each pair is going to make one puppet. It can be a pet, a farm animal, an animal from the jungle, or even an insect.
	3 If necessary, show them how to make the puppet. Then give them about 15 minutes to make their puppet.
	4 Draw up a personal file on the board (see the file card) and get the children to recall the information for your puppet.

5 Tell each pair to invent a similar personal file for their puppet.

6 Ask them what questions they need to ask to get the information in the personal file, and if necessary practise them.

7 Tell the children that they are going to find out about the other puppets in the class and report back.

8 One child in each pair takes the puppet, the other finds another puppet to talk to. You could involve writing in this activity by getting them to fill in personal files for the puppets they interview, or you could tell them to remember as much information as possible and report back at the end. Give the children time to talk to two or three puppets. Then the children with puppets change with those without puppets and the activity is repeated.

FOLLOW-UP

The children report back to their partner and class what they have found out and decide which animal they like most.

VARIATIONS

The puppets can be pop, film, or sports stars. In this case the children can stick a photo of their hero on the puppet for the face. They could also be aliens or monsters.

5 Short plays

There are six short plays in this chapter (activities 5.19–5.24). Some of them are suitable for young children in their first year of English, and others are aimed at older children who have been studying English for longer. All the plays are easy to stage and fun to act, and children will find working together on a play motivating and memorable.

The chapter starts with notes on each step of preparing a play followed by a variety of activities for each step. Then there is a short introduction to each play and a brief guide to preparing it. The texts of the plays are in the photocopiable playscripts at the end of the book.

Preparing a play

The basic steps for preparing a play are:

- introducing the characters and telling the story;
- introducing the dialogue;
- casting and character building;
- learning the lines and rehearsing;
- reflecting and giving feedback;
- the final rehearsal;
- the props and costumes;
- the performance.

These steps are flexible, and of course you can adapt them to suit your circumstances. In the next section you will find ideas and activities for each step.

Plays tell stories but you can also use them to introduce cross-curricular material—ideas from other subjects such as Geography or History—or you can make them part of work on issues which run through the curriculum, like pollution and health education. When preparing a play you work on many aspects of English as well as other more general aspects of education, working together co-operatively, or allowing reflection and self-evaluation by the children. In most cases, the preparation of a play, or the 'process', is more important than the final performance, the 'product', though this should not be devalued. Children get great enjoyment and satisfaction from performing a play. You can also produce plays for a wider public: other classes in the school, parents, or for school open days. The children will find it easier if they have done some of the activities in the previous chapters, which introduce them to acting on a smaller scale.

You can ask the children to write their own plays. This is motivating for them, and will encourage them to draw on all the language they know. They can make up their own versions of a play they have worked on or dramatize stories that they have read or invented.

Introducing the characters and telling the story

5.1 Telling the story with puppets

LEVEL	**All**
AGE GROUP	**All**
TIME	**10–15 minutes, depending on the length of the story.**
AIMS	**Language:** to listen to a story. **Other:** to introduce characters and story in preparation for a play.
DESCRIPTION	The teacher tells the story of the play using puppets as the characters.
MATERIALS	Puppets like those in Chapter 3.

PREPARATION

1 Decide which kind of puppet you are going to use (see Chapter 4). 'Stick puppets' are good, especially if you are going to put on a performance.
2 Make a puppet yourself for each character.
3 Find or make any props you will need. For example, in 'Marty the Martian' you will need a bar of chocolate, an ice cream, some biscuits, and a cauliflower.
4 Practise the story.

IN CLASS

1 Introduce the characters and use them to help you tell the story. It may be difficult to use the puppets as puppets here, as you might not have enough hands. However, you can use them as flashcards, sticking them to the board for each scene.
2 Check that the children have understood the story by getting them to tell you what happened as you point at the puppets.

5.2 Using a board picture

LEVEL	**All**
AGE GROUP	**All**
TIME	**15–20 minutes, depending on the length of the story.**
AIMS	**Language:** listening to a story. **Other:** introduce children to the characters and storyline of a play they are going to perform.
DESCRIPTION	The teacher tells the story of the play, using a board picture to help her.
MATERIALS	A board, and something with which to stick the pictures on, for example: blu-tack, magnets, or velcro.

PREPARATION

1 Make cut-out figures of the characters you need.
2 Sketch the picture you are going to use on the board, this is particularly useful when the story involves a journey like 'Chicken Little' (see 5.20, 'Chicken Little').
3 Practise the story.

IN CLASS

1 Introduce the characters. Stick them on the picture in the positions they appear in the story.
2 Tell the story, moving the characters as necessary.

VARIATION

You can draw a plan of the stage on the board and use this to tell the story. This is useful in a play like 'That's Funny' (see 5.23) where the stage is divided into three areas and they are used for different scenes (see page 84).

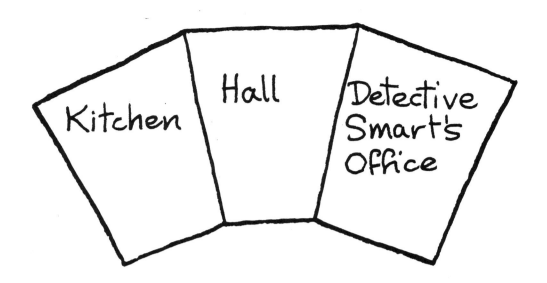

5.3   Picture cues

LEVEL	**All**
AGE GROUP	**All**
TIME	**15–20 minutes, depending on the length of the story.**
AIMS	**Language:** language of suggestion; listening to a story. **Other:** preparing the children for a play they are going to perform.
DESCRIPTION	The teacher uses key pictures, for example, a pumpkin and a glass slipper, to help her tell the story of a play the children are going to perform.
MATERIALS	Pictures from the story.
PREPARATION	1 Decide on the pictures you need to elicit the story from the children. If you are using a well-known story like 'Cinderella' (see 5.21), then one key picture is enough—for example, a pumpkin.
IN CLASS	1 Draw or stick the first picture on the board. Tell the children it is from a well-known fairy-tale and get them to guess which one. Put them into pairs and get them to discuss their ideas.
	2 Elicit their answers and tell them the right one.
	3 Elicit the rest of the characters for the story.
	4 Either tell the story in English or ask the children to tell you the story first in their language.

5.4   What happens next?

LEVEL	**2, 3**
AGE GROUP	**All**
TIME	**20 minutes**
AIMS	**Language:** language of speculation; listening to a story in order to guess what will happen next. **Other:** to prepare the children for performing a play.
PREPARATION	1 Decide on suitable points in the story to stop—for example, at a point of suspense, and ask *What is going to happen?* A good story for this kind of activity is 'That's Funny' (see 5.23). 2 Practise telling the story.
IN CLASS	1 Introduce the characters and start to tell the story. When you reach the first stopping point, ask the children to tell you what is going to happen, particularly when something exciting is about to happen. Accept all their suggestions and then continue. 2 Stop again and ask them which of their suggestions were correct. Then continue until the next stopping point.

Introducing the dialogue

It is important to introduce the dialogue to the whole class before giving individual children their parts. This helps to set the story in the children's minds and reduces the amount that they have to learn later on. You can introduce the dialogue scene-by-scene, or you can present the children with the whole play at once. Many of the suggestions in this section are for children who can read. If you are working with children who cannot read in English yet, then you will need to introduce and practise the dialogue with the whole class together. There are suggestions for helping individual children remember their lines in the section 'Learning the lines and rehearsing'.

5.5   Listen to the play

LEVEL	**All**
AGE GROUP	**All**
TIME	**About 15, but depends on the length of the play.**
MATERIALS	A tape recording of the play you are using.

| AIMS | **Language:** listening generally to a story, and for specific information. |
| | **Other:** to introduce the dialogue of a play which children are going to perform. |

| DESCRIPTION | The teacher plays a recording of the play and gives the children a task to do so that they become familiar with the dialogue. |

PREPARATION

1 If you can, find people who will record the play on cassette for you.
2 Prepare a task for the children to do while they are listening: for example, some pictures to order, a table to complete, phrases to listen out for, matching character to words, or any other suitable listening comprehension task.

IN CLASS

1 Go through the story, eliciting what happens from the children.
2 Explain the comprehension task to the children.
3 Play the cassette, or read out the play, and give the children time to do the task. Play the cassette again.
4 Check the children's answers with them.

5.6 Mixed-up lines

| LEVEL | **All** |

| AGE GROUP | **All** |

| TIME | **20–30 minutes** |

| AIMS | **Language:** practise reading skills: word recognition. |
| | **Other:** to introduce the dialogue of a play before rehearsing it. |

| MATERIALS | Flashcards with the lines of the dialogue written on them; flashcards with pictures of the characters, or puppets. |

| DESCRIPTION | This technique is suitable for plays that have a simple basic dialogue that is repeated with variations as the play unfolds, for example, 'Marty the Martian' (see 5.19). |

PREPARATION

1 Write each line of the dialogue in big letters on a flashcard.
2 Draw pictures of the characters on the board, or make flashcards or puppets.

IN CLASS

1 Use the pictures or puppets to demonstrate the dialogue.
2 Stick up the lines of the dialogue on the board and ask the children to put them in the right order.
3 Ask the children to practise them in pairs.

4 Turn one of the lines over and ask the children to practise the dialogue again.

5 Continue turning the lines over until the children can 'read' the blank lines.

VARIATION

If your children can't read English, prepare picture cues for each line.

5.7 Repeat to a rhythm

LEVEL

All

AGE GROUP

All

TIME

20 minutes

AIMS

Language: to practise stress and rhythm.
Other: to encourage memorization, to introduce a part of a play before rehearsing it.

MATERIALS

Percussion instruments and a poster of the chant (optional).

DESCRIPTION

This activity is useful to teach chants or dialogues with a strong rhythm, for example the chants in 'Chicken Little' (see 5.20).

PREPARATION

1 Establish the rhythm of the chant and practise it by clicking your fingers or clapping your hands in time.

2 (Optional) Find percussion instruments for the children to use while they are chanting.

3 If your children can read, you may like to make a poster of the chant.

IN CLASS

1 Teach the children the rhythm of the chant and get them to clap it, or bang their percussion instruments in time.

2 Chant the chant and get the children to accompany you.

3 Teach the chant line by line, and finally get the children to chant it all the way through.

VARIATION

Divide the children into groups after step 1. Ask each group to practise the rhythm using 'body percussion', for example, by clicking their fingers, stamping their feet, and slapping their thighs.

5.8   Predict the lines

LEVEL	2, 3
AGE GROUP	B, C
TIME	**15 minutes for a short piece of dialogue, but it depends how much of the dialogue you are going to do this way.**
AIMS	**Language:** getting the children to use their entire language resource to choose appropriate language for a situation. **Other:** building the dialogue for use in a play.
DESCRIPTION	This activity is useful with children with a higher level of English. Although they may not predict exactly the same words as the script, you should accept their version unless your aims call for the exact language of the text.
IN CLASS	1 Set the context of the scene, for example, *Cinderella is sitting in the kitchen; she is crying.*
	2 Explain what happens, for example, *The rats come up to her.* Ask the children what the rats say and how Cinderella replies. Build up the dialogue on the board.

5.9   Match the dialogue to the character

LEVEL	2, 3
AGE GROUP	B, C
TIME	**20 minutes, but it depends on the amount of dialogue you select.**
AIMS	**Language:** associating words with character and style. **Other:** learning a dialogue.
DESCRIPTION	This activity is useful when the characters are clearly defined, for example in fairy-tales.
IN CLASS	1 Ask the children to recall the characters in the play.
	2 Write the dialogue from a scene on the board. Ask the children to match the characters to the lines they say.

5.10 Fill the gaps

LEVEL	2, 3
AGE GROUP	B, C
TIME	**30 minutes, but it depends on the amount of dialogue you have selected.**

AIMS — **Language:** getting children to use their entire linguistic knowledge to select appropriate language for a situation.
Other: to introduce dialogue for a play.

PREPARATION

1 Prepare the script you will put on the board. Write the name of the character, and then dashes to represent the number of words in the line. For scene 6 in 'Cinderella' (see Worksheet 5.21), you would have:

```
Prince        ____  ____  ____
Stepsister 1  ____  ____
Stepsister 2  ____  ____
Prince        ____  ____  ____  ____
Rats 1 and 2  ____  ____  ____  ____
```

IN CLASS

1 Explain the context of the scene. In this scene the Prince is looking for the owner of the shoe.

2 Ask the children what they think each character says. If they guess a word correctly, write it in all the spaces it appears in (you may need to give them some clues).

3 Continue until they have completed as much of the dialogue as possible and then give them the remaining words.

5.11 Find the rhyme

LEVEL	2, 3
AGE GROUP	B, C
TIME	**30 minutes**

AIMS — **Language:** to raise awareness of the phonology of words, particularly 'rhyme'.
Other: to introduce children to the dialogue of a play that rhymes.

MATERIALS — Correction fluid for blanking out the rhyming words.

DESCRIPTION

The teacher prepares the text from a rhyming play, such as 'Find a bin to put it in' (5.22), by blanking out the rhyming words. The children become familiar with the dialogue and rhythm by filling in the gaps.

PREPARATION

1   Make a copy of the text and white out the rhyming words to make a gapped text.
2   Make a list of the rhyming words, in two groups, with one word from each rhyming pair in each group.

IN CLASS

1   Remind the children of the story and the characters.
2   Write the rhyming words on the board in two columns, out of order. In 'Find a bin to put it in' (5.22), these would be:

> white friends eat please go bag skin sight stink
> think right bright tin ends rag Pete know cheese

3   Ask the children to match the rhyming words from each column.
4   Give out the gapped texts. Explain which lines rhyme and ask them to complete the text with the words from the board.
5   Read the text aloud so that the children can check their work.

5.12   Matching lines to summaries

LEVEL

3

AGE GROUP

B, C

TIME

20 minutes or more, depending on the length of the play.

AIMS

Language: reading: following the logical structure of a story; comparing spoken and written text.
Other: to familiarize children with the story and dialogue of a play.

PREPARATION

1   Prepare a mixed-up series of summaries or pictures of each scene. Make copies for the children.
2   Prepare a copy of the script. Make copies for the children.

IN CLASS

1   Ask the children to recall the story and then give out the summaries. Get them to put them in order.
2   Give out the copies of the scripts. Ask the children to work in pairs and match the scripts to the summaries.

Casting and character building

It is important to make sure that all the children participate in the play, whatever their abilities or circumstances. In a class you may well have children with different language levels and abilities, and you could have children with special needs too. You can improvise non-speaking roles or ask children with particular artistic or organizational abilities to be in charge of scenery, props, posters, and programme design. There are three basic possibilities for assigning roles:

1 You, the teacher, decide which child plays which part, taking into account the character and language abilities of each child.
2 The children decide on the roles themselves, volunteering for specific parts, or suggesting their classmates for different characters.
3 The casting is done at random: write the parts on slips of paper and each child draws one.

Each method has its advantages and drawbacks. Some of the factors you need to take into account when deciding how to cast are:
 — the children's maturity;
 — the relationship they have with you and each other;
 — whether the quality of the performance is important or if it is really the process of preparing it that interests you;
 — whether you want to give certain children a chance to 'shine'.

Once the casting has been done, you may like to help the children make the character their own. Some ways of doing this are outlined in this section.

5.13 Gestures and walks

LEVEL	1, 2
AGE GROUP	**All**
TIME	**10 minutes**
AIMS	**Language:** associating language with physical movement (Total Physical Response). **Other:** introducing children to the characters in a play.
DESCRIPTION	This is suitable for a play like 'Chicken Little' (5.20) where each character has a well-defined personality.

IN CLASS	1 Elicit the story and the characters from the children.
	2 Ask the children to suggest a gesture for each character. For example, for a hen you can bend your arms, hold them close to your sides, and flap them. Then ask the children how each character would walk. For example, a hen moves its head backwards and forwards.
	3 Call out the names of the characters and the children respond with the appropriate gesture and walk.

5.14   Mime and guess

LEVEL	**All**
AGE GROUP	**All**
TIME	**10–15 minutes**
AIMS	**Language:** association of words with physical actions (Total Physical Response). **Other:** helping children to create a picture in their minds of the character they are to play.
DESCRIPTION	The children create typical actions for the characters in the play and act them out.
IN CLASS	1 Ask the children to remember and tell you the story and who the characters are.
	2 Ask the children to mime a gesture or action typical of each character. For example in 'Cinderella' (see 5.21), the stepmother looks bad-tempered and claps her hands together giving orders.
	3 The children work in groups. One child mimes a character and the others guess.

5.15   Make your own role card

LEVEL	2, 3
AGE GROUP	**All**
TIME	**10–15 minutes**
AIMS	**Language:** adjectives, language for talking about someone's character, for example: likes and dislikes. **Other:** helping children to create a picture in their minds of the role they are to play.

DESCRIPTION   The children make role cards for the characters they are playing, including likes and dislikes, jobs, and so on.

PREPARATION   Make a basic role card like the one here for each of the children.

ROLE CARD

Name _____

Age _____

Appearance _____

Clothes _____

Character _____

Photocopiable © Oxford University Press

IN CLASS

1 Elicit the story and the characters and distribute the roles.
2 Give out the blank role cards and ask the children to complete them for their character. You may like all the children who are playing the same character to work together.

Learning the lines and rehearsing

None of the plays in this book has large parts which require the children to memorize a lot of lines. The context often suggests the dialogue, and so the children do not really have to learn the lines, but rather supply language suitable to the situation. This close connection between context and language, helps them remember what they need to say. However, at lower levels improvisation is difficult as the children do not have the necessary language resources, so the lines give them support and confidence. You must make it clear to the children that you are not asking them to be word perfect, but that they should do the best they can. If you take time to rehearse the scenes and suggest strategies for learning their lines, the children do not usually have problems with remembering what they have to say.

If you are opposed on principle to getting children to learn their lines, they can note them down on a small piece of paper and read them from it. The drawback is that a lot of spontaneity of action is lost when the children read.

Useful strategies for learning lines

- practise reading the dialogue with a friend;
- cover parts of the dialogue and practise it with a friend, for example: cover the first word or two of each line with a piece of

paper and practise the dialogue, then gradually increase the number of words covered up;

– read the dialogue three times with a friend, the first time looking at the script, the second 'half looking', and third not looking at all. 'Half looking' means that they try not to look at the text, but have it in front of them to look at if necessary;
– practise saying the dialogue in your head;
– practise saying the dialogue under your breath (muttering);
– write down your part several times;
– sing or say the dialogue with a marked rhythm;
– visualize the dialogue: imagine a series of pictures, one for each line and associate the words with the pictures.

When the children are familiar with their lines, they can act out the scenes. The acting should be kept as simple as possible: the children need to know where and when to enter and exit, and how to move on stage. They can decide this themselves, or you can direct them. This will depend on how much experience they have of acting, and how much freedom you wish to let them have.

5.16   What to say and when to say it

LEVEL	2, 3
AGE GROUP	B, C
TIME	**20–30 minutes, but it depends on the length of the play.**
AIMS	**Language:** practising language before you produce it. **Other:** to help children become familiar with their lines and when they have to say them.
DESCRIPTION	The children identify their own lines in the script, as well as those of the character before them. They read the script.
MATERIALS	Copies of the script.
PREPARATION	Make a copy of the script for each child.
IN CLASS	1 Explain to the children that they need to know their own lines and when to say them. This means they need to listen for the line before theirs.

2 Put all the children playing the same part together. Give out the scripts and ask the children to underline their own lines with a continuous line, and the line before theirs with a dotted line or with a different coloured pen.

3 Rearrange the children in groups with one of each character. Ask them to read the play.

5.17   From choral to individual

LEVEL	1, 2
AGE GROUP	All
TIME	20 minutes, but it depends how much practice you think is necessary
AIMS	**Language:** choral drilling of language to provide a model and to provide an opportunity for practising accuracy before speaking alone. **Other:** to help the children learn their lines.
DESCRIPTION	The children practise saying the dialogue chorally before reading the play and saying their own lines.
IN CLASS	1 Put all the children playing the same character together. Read through the play. All the children playing the same character read out the lines together in chorus. 2 Ask the children to turn the texts over and try going through the play in chorus again. Repeat this step as often as you feel necessary. 3 Finally, put the children in groups with one of each character and ask them to say the play through.

5.18   Catch, speak, and throw

LEVEL	1, 2
AGE GROUP	A, B
TIME	20 minutes
AIMS	**Language:** to follow a predictable pattern in a dialogue. **Other:** to help children learn their lines.
DESCRIPTION	This activity is useful when the characters speak in a predictable order, for example, Scene 2 of 'Cinderella' (see playscript 5.21).
MATERIALS	A soft ball or ball of paper.
IN CLASS	1 If there are three characters in the scene, draw a triangle on the board and write the name of each character on the corners. Then write the dialogue round the triangle, or use pictures as prompts. See the triangle for Scene 2 in 'Cinderella' (playscript 5.21), for example.

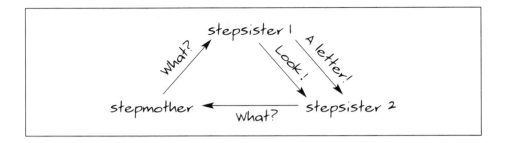

2 Divide the class into three groups, one for each character, and ask each group to choose a 'catcher'. Tell them that when the catcher catches the ball, the others in the group should say their character's line.

3 Start throwing the ball like this:

Stepsister 1 Look.   (Throws the ball to Stepsister 2)
Stepsister 2 What?   (Throws the ball to Stepmother)
Stepmother What?   (Throws the ball to Stepsister 1)
Stepsister 1 A letter! (Throws the ball to Stepsister 2)

4 Regroup the children in groups of three, with one of each character, to practise the scene again.

Reflection and feedback

Reflection and feedback on the children's performance in rehearsals are very important, especially if the children are not used to acting. After rehearsing, you should give the children time to think about their work. This reflection may be done in groups or as a whole class. It may be oral or written. The children should think about key points, evaluate themselves, and consider how they could improve. You can also give your opinion: it is good practice to concentrate on positive points as this will reinforce your criteria of a good performance and help the whole class understand what they are aiming to achieve.

You watched each other and gave some useful suggestions.
Next time, try to change over groups faster.
You spoke clearly.
You need to listen to each other.

Make a note of both your and the children's comments, and use it to remind the children of their conclusions at the beginning of the next session. If you feel the children's reflections have been especially useful, you can make a poster of the main points and put it on the classroom wall for future reference.

Feedback is probably best done in the children's own language as they will be able to express themselves more precisely. Remember that the aim of this activity is not language but to help the children think about their performance and how to improve it.

Some ways of conducting feedback and reflection

Oral
- Ask the children to talk in small groups and agree on two or three things they like about their work and one thing that could be improved.
- Ask the children to think about their performance and say which are the three most important factors to remember for a good performance.
- Ask the children to say a sentence using this framework:

  We did … well/better, because …

Written
- Prepare a short questionnaire which focuses on important points (speaking clearly, entrances/exits, knowing lines, being quiet backstage, looking at the person you are speaking to, and so on). Ask the group to complete it, and decide where they do well and where they need to improve.
- Ask the group to write a list of three pieces of advice they would give to another group doing the same activity.
- Ask the group to write sentences about themselves or another group, starting:

  I like the way … , because …

EXAMPLES

PUPPETS Watch the scenes and answer the questions.	Scene 1	Scene 2	Scene 3	Scene 4
1 Did they hold the puppets up high enough?				
2 Did the puppets look at each other?				
3 Did the puppets move too much?				
4 Did they know where to enter and exit from?				
5 Did they speak loudly and clearly?				
6 How can they improve?				

Photocopiable © Oxford University Press

ACTORS

1 Do you know your lines?

2 Do you know when to speak?

3 Do you know where to enter and exit?

4 Do you know how to move on stage?

5 Do you speak loudly enough?

6 Do you listen to the others on stage?

Photocopiable © Oxford University Press

BACKSTAGE BEHAVIOUR

1 Do you keep quiet when other children are on stage?

2 Do you keep still when other children are on stage?

3 Do you watch the others and think about their performance?

4 Do you know which side of the stage you should wait on?

5 Do you know where your props are?

Photocopiable © Oxford University Press

The final rehearsal

This often requires patience and a certain amount of organizational skill on the part of the teacher. A degree of noise and disorganization is to be expected, especially if several groups are rehearsing at the same time. However, you can reduce this by having a detailed plan of action and organizing as much as possible in advance. You may also need to use diplomatic skills with your colleagues, warning them in advance to expect more noise than usual. It is worth considering alternatives to having two or more groups rehearsing at a time: you may be able to use another classroom, or you could consider rehearsing one group at a time while the others do written work.

If the play is for the general public, you should try to rehearse the whole play at least twice, with time for reflection and feedback between the two rehearsals. If you are going to use props and costumes, the second rehearsal should be a dress rehearsal, with the children wearing their costumes and using the props (see below). It is useful to video the final rehearsal, and give feedback before the final performance.

Props and costumes

Props (objects that are used in the play—umbrellas, books, cups and so on) and costumes should be kept very simple. You can decide on the costumes, or you can ask the children for their suggestions. Some ideas are:

- sandwich boards of paper: these are cheap and easy to make (see picture);

- headbands or half-masks can give a character its identity (see Chapter 3);
- add a single item like gloves or jewellery to a basic costume of jeans and T-shirt.

Make sure that each child knows what they are wearing and has a specific place to keep his or her costume. Similarly, each child should be responsible for their own props. It may be useful to have a large box near the performing area to keep the props in.

The performance

Having spent time on preparing the play, it is important that the children give at least one performance. But this does not need to be in a formal setting or with an outside public. The children can show their play to the other children in their class or to other children in the school. This is motivating for the actors and the audience: the actors get a lot of satisfaction and self-esteem out of a performance and the audience sees what can be done with English. You can make the performance as much of an event as you wish: you may like to prepare posters, issue invitations, and prepare programmes. On the other hand, it can be low-key with none of these things. The children usually appreciate it if you take photos and display them later. If you have access to a video camera, you can film the play and use it for feedback in later lessons.

The plays

Six plays are presented in activities 5.19 to 5.24 of this section. There are notes which describe the play and then a sequence of activities that build up to a performance of it. The activities themselves are not described in detail, but you can select the ones that are best for your class from the previous section. The photocopiable playscripts appear at the back of the book.

The order of the plays is roughly from the simplest to the most difficult, in terms of language. Three are constructed around a basic dialogue which changes slightly in each scene. In 'Cinderella' (5.21) the dialogue is reduced to the minimum, 'Find a Bin' (5.22) is in verse, and the last play (5.24, 'Starlet') is reminiscent of TV advertisements. If you don't find the play you are looking for here, you may like to take one of these as a model and use it to write your own. You can also use the plays as the starting point for children to write their own texts. There are two ideas for doing this at the end of the chapter.

5.19   Marty the Martian

LEVEL	1, 2
AGE GROUP	A
TIME	**40 minutes to tell the story and make the puppets; 2 × 40 minutes for the play.**
AIMS	**Language:** likes and dislikes, suggestions. **Other:** working together on a play.
DESCRIPTION	This is a very simple play with a repetitive structure.
MATERIALS	Materials for puppets and theatre, if you are using them, see Chapter 3; photocopies of the script (Worksheet 5.19).
PREPARATION	1 Make your puppets to tell the story. 2 Make a theatre (see 3.9, 'Simple puppet theatres').
IN CLASS	1 Tell the story using the puppets. 2 Divide the children into groups of six to make their puppets. 3 Teach the dialogue and get the children to practise it in pairs. 4 Tell the story again; encourage the children to join in. 5 (Optional) If the children can read, and you feel they need the support of the written script, give them the playscript and ask them to underline their parts.

6 Rehearse the play. While the others watch they complete a
   feedback form.

7 Give feedback and rehearse again.

8 The groups show each other their plays.

COMMENTS   You can omit some of the characters and vary the language to suit
                             your class.

5.20 Chicken Little

LEVEL   2, 3

AGE GROUP   **A, B**

TIME   **6 × 30 minutes plus rehearsal and performance, or 15 minute
                             slots over twelve lessons.**

AIMS   **Language:** prepositions, *must*, past simple.
                             Other: group dynamics and co-ordination.

DESCRIPTION   This is a play based on an American folk tale adapted from Carolyn
                             Graham's *Jazz Chant Fairytales*.

MATERIALS   Photocopies of the script (Worksheet 5.20); materials for props (see
                             Chapter 3).

PREPARATION   1 Read the script
                             2 Practise the sketch map of the route the animals take.

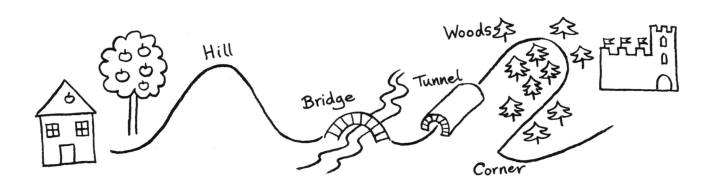

                             3 Make cut-out pictures of the characters.

IN CLASS   1 Draw a sketch map of the route the animals take and use cut-out
                                pictures to tell the story.
                             2 Teach the first chant and practise it.

3 Teach the second chant and practise it. The children can accompany the chant with percussion instruments (see 5.7, 'Repeat to a rhythm').

4 Work on a gesture to represent each character, and a walk for each one. Practise them together with the second chant (see 5.13, 'Gestures and walks').

5 Work on gestures for 'up the hill' and so on. The children practise these gestures in role.

6 (Optional) The children make masks for their characters (see 3.12, 'Masks').

7 Teach the dialogue and practise it.

8 Divide the children into groups with the same number of children as there are characters in the play. Each child chooses a role. Each group rehearses its own version of the play. Watch and give feedback to individual groups.

9 The groups show each other their work.

10 Allow reflection and feedback on the whole process.

COMMENTS

If you want to vary the number of roles for the children, you can increase the number of children in the chorus. You can play the narrator yourself, or you can give different parts of the role to different children. I learnt about this play from Amaya Arribi, Susi Díaz, and Elena de la Inglesia.

5.21   Cinderella

LEVEL

2, 3

AGE GROUP

All

TIME

10 × 30 minutes plus

AIMS

Language: various structures, including: possessives, questions, and instructions; following a script.
Other: group co-ordination, motivation, fun.

DESCRIPTION

This is an example of a play where most of the lines have between one and three words. This makes them easier for the children to learn, but acting has to carry a lot of the meaning.

MATERIALS

Photocopies of the script (Worksheet 5.21); materials for props (see Chapter 3).

PREPARATION

Read through the script.

IN CLASS

1 Draw a pumpkin on the board and ask the children which fairy story it comes from. Elicit the characters and the story (see 5.3, 'Picture cues').

2 Work on gestures for each character. One child mimes a character, while the others guess who it is (see 5.14, 'Mime and guess').

3 Introduce the scenes one by one, and practise them. For example:

Scene 1: Make flashcards of the dialogue, the children order them (see 5.6, 'Mixed-up lines').

Scene 2: Draw a triangle on the board, build up the dialogue round it. The children practise the dialogue as they throw a ball (see 5.18, 'Catch, speak, and throw').

Scenes 3 and 4: Teach the children some basic expressions. Give them the context and ask them to predict the dialogue (see 5.8, 'Predict the lines'), then practise it.

Scene 5: Write the lines on the board. Ask the children to match the lines to the characters (see 5.9, 'Match the dialogue to the character'). Practise the dialogue.

Scene 6: Set the context, and then do a gap-fill activity (see 5.10, 'Fill the gaps'). Practise the dialogue.

4 Divide the children who are performing the play into groups of nine, with each group containing all the characters from the play. It is easier to rehearse if you have two children playing Cinderella.

5 Divide each group of nine into two:

Group 1	Group 2
Stepmother Stepsister 1 Stepsister 2 Cinderella A	Cinderella B Rat 1 Rat 2 Fairy Godmother Prince

6 Give the children a feedback form (such as the first form on page 98) to complete for their own scenes.

7 Rehearse the play.

Scene 1	Scene 2	Scene 3	Scene 4	Scene 5	Scene 6
Stepmother Stepsister 1 Stepsister 2 Cinderella A	Stepmother Stepsister 1 Stepsister 2	Stepmother Stepsister 1 Stepsister 2 Cinderella A Fairy Godmother	Cinderella A Cinderella B Rat 1 Rat 2	Cinderella B Rat 1 Rat 2 Fairy Godmother Prince Stepsister 1 Stepsister 2	Stepmother Cinderella A Rat 1 Rat 2 Fairy Godmother Prince Stepsister 1 Stepsister 2

- Group 1 can rehearse scenes 1 and 3 while Group 2 rehearses scene 5, apart from the Stepsisters' dialogue.
- Group 1, without Cinderella A, rehearses scene 2 while Group 2, with Cinderella A and B, rehearses scene 4.
- Everybody can rehearse scene 6 together.

8 Decide on the costumes and props (for ideas see Chapter 3).

9 Conduct a full dress rehearsal of the play. Give the children who are not acting something to do while they are waiting their turn to rehearse.

10 The groups of nine perform their version of the play for each other.

11 Ask the children to reflect on the experience and draw some conclusions.

COMMENTS

If you need to vary the number of characters, Rat 1 and Rat 2 can be played by one child, and you can also add characters at the Ball. I suggest that you work on one scene per lesson with all the children and do not cast the characters until the end of the preparation period.

5.22   Find a bin to put it in

LEVEL

2, 3

AGE GROUP

B, C

TIME

4 × 30 minutes

AIMS

Language: language about the environment, rhyming words, adjectives.
Other: group co-ordination and fun.

DESCRIPTION

This is a short play in verse which carries a message about caring for the environment. There is a basic cast of six characters and a narrator. This play can be performed by children or with stick puppets. The activities suggested below are for puppets; there are photocopiable outlines for the puppets in Worksheet 5.22.

There are four steps to preparing the play, as, unlike the other plays, the children do not need to work intensively on the dialogue or learn it by heart.

MATERIALS

Photocopies of playscript 5.22; puppets and theatre (see Chapter 3); a bag, a fizzy drinks can, a tin, a banana skin, a dirty rag, silver foil; long sticks of wire; sticky tape.

PREPARATION

1 Read the story.

2 Make puppets if you are using them.

3 Prepare a gap-fill text (see 5.11, 'Find the rhyme').

IN CLASS

1 Use puppets and 'rubbish' to tell the story.

2 Write the rhyming words on the board. When the children have made rhyming pairs of words use them to complete the gap-fill text (see 5.11, 'Find the rhyme'). The completed texts will be used in step 4.

3 Divide the children into groups of six (or as many as you have in the play). Tell them to make the puppets (Chapter 3). They will also need to put the rubbish on a long stick or wire, so that they can 'fly' it through the air (see the picture).

4 Practise the play using the texts from step 2. The children can stick these at eye level inside their puppet theatre.

5 Give the children a feedback form to fill in.

6 Rehearse the play again.

7 Each group shows its play to the class.

COMMENTS

You can vary the number of mermaids and mermen if you need to.

5.23 That's funny

LEVEL

3

AGE GROUP

C

TIME

3 × 50 minute lessons, or 6 × 20–30 minutes over different lessons.

AIMS

Language: the present perfect, modals of speculation.
Other: working on cross-curricular themes: music (a rap) and craft (making instruments).

DESCRIPTION   This play is a detective story with two familiar characters, the detective who thinks he knows everything and his assistant who finally resolves the case. There are ten characters in the cast; three of these are children. The number of children can be increased or decreased as necessary.

MATERIALS   Photocopies of playscript 5.23; materials for making percussion 'instruments': balloons, beans, yoghurt pots, elastic bands, empty shoe boxes, and blocks of wood.

PREPARATION
1 Learn the rap.
2 Make a percussion instrument to demonstrate.

IN CLASS
1 Teach the first verse of the rap and the vocabulary needed to make the instruments.
2 Tell the children to make percussion instruments (see 5.7, 'Repeat to a rhythm').
3 Teach the rest of the rap and practise it with the percussion instruments.
4 Draw the division of the stage on the board (see the illustration in 5.2, 'Using a board picture'). Tell the story, stopping at intervals and asking the children to predict what is going to happen (see 5.8, 'Predict the lines'). Do not tell them the end, but ask them to predict who was taking the things and why.
5 Divide the children into groups of ten and cast the roles. Give out the scripts. The children read them to check their predictions and underline their parts.
6 Teach the children the basic dialogue.
7 Divide each group like this:

Group A	Group B
Nicky	Al
Jerry	Pat
Det. Smart	Child 2
Slow	Child 3
Child 1	Child 4

Group A can practise Scenes 1, 3, and 5 with Child 1 as prompter. Group B can practise Scenes 2 and 4. Child 2 can take the role of Detective Smart and Child 3 the role of Slow; Child 4 acts as prompter.
8 Practise scene 6 all together.
9 Decide on the costumes and make them or collect them (see Chapter 3 for ideas).
10 Each group rehearses their play and completes a feedback sheet (see page 98).
11 The groups show each other their plays.

5.24 Starlet

LEVEL	3
AGE GROUP	C
TIME	**3 × 50 minute lessons**

AIMS

Language: using conversational language and colloquial phrases.
Other: working as a group, the performance.

DESCRIPTION

This play tells the story of an ordinary girl or boy, Starlet, who becomes a film star through a series of strange coincidences. There are eleven short scenes, each showing a step in Starlet's path to stardom. Starlet and the Film Director move from one scene to the next while the other characters remain still when they are not acting (see Worksheet 5.24).

MATERIALS

Copies of Worksheet 5.24 (a) and (b), copies of Playscript 5.24, and role cards like those in 5.15.

PREPARATION

1 Read the play.
2 Photocopy Playscript 5.24, Worksheets 5.24 (a) and 5.24 (b).
3 Photocopy role cards like those on 5.15.

IN CLASS

1 Tell the children to match the summary sentences to the flow chart on the worksheet.
2 Ask them to match the dialogues to the flow chart and summary sentences on the worksheets.
3 Cast the play and give out role cards for the children to complete for each character (see photocopiable role card in 5.15).
4 Put the children into pairs to learn their parts.
5 Put them into groups with one of each character. Each group draws the boxes of the flow chart on the floor and practises each scene in the appropriate box.
6 Each group watches the others rehearse and gives feedback.
7 The children rehearse again, taking into account the feedback.
8 The children show each other their final versions.

COMMENTS

– The number of characters is variable. One child can play two characters, or the number of characters can be increased by writing more scenes.
– When you have done this play with the children, they can use it as a model to write similar ones themselves.
– This is a good play for videoing. The short film can be used for feedback.

GLOSSARY OF PLAY WORDS

act (n): a section of a play, longer than a scene. It usually finishes when something dramatic happens.

act (v): to perform a part in a play or film.

cast (n): the group of actors acting in a play.

cast (v): to choose which actor will play which part.

dress rehearsal: practising the play with all the costumes and props.

lines: the dialogue in a play.

narrator: someone who tells the audience what is happening, or the background to the plot.

prompter: someone who reminds the actors when they forget their lines.

props: items that the actors use on stage—an umbrella, a basket, and so on.

rehearse: to practise a play.

rehearsal: the act of practising a play.

scene: a time of continuous action which usually all takes place in the same place; for example, the scene in the kitchen in 'Cinderella' (see 5.21).

scenery: the pieces of furniture and decoration on stage.

script: the text of a play.

stage: place where the actors stand.

5.25 Using a model to write a play

LEVEL	2, 3
AGE GROUP	B, C
TIME	2 × 50 minute lessons to write the play; another 2 × 50 minutes to rehearse and perform it.
AIMS	**Language:** to practise writing following a model. **Other:** to develop the children's creativity in English.
DESCRIPTION	The children write a play of their own, using one they have already worked on as a model.
MATERIALS	Copies of the script of the original play for each group of three of four.
PREPARATION	Choose a play which is suitable for your class to use as a model. You could use one from this book or one you have written yourself. The children should be familiar with it.
IN CLASS	1 Remind the children of the play that you are going to use as a model. Ask them to suggest how they could change it (the characters, the setting of the story, the ending). Write their suggestions on the board.

2   Divide the children into groups of three or four. Tell each group that it is going to write a play.

3   Give the children the text and explain that they are going to use it as the skeleton of their play, but that they need to change the words to fit in with their new story.

4   Give the children time to work on their play. Go around the groups helping with language and making suggestions where necessary.

5   When the children have finished writing, they prepare their new version of the play for the others to see.

FOLLOW-UP   The children give feedback on each other's plays.

COMMENTS   You can do this as a whole-class activity. The children make suggestions for the new dialogue and you write them on the board to build up the new script.

5.26   Superheroes: writing a play from an idea

LEVEL   2, 3

AGE GROUP   B, C

TIME   1–2 × 50 minute to write the play; 2 × 50 minutes to rehearse and perform it.

AIMS   **Language:** to practise writing dialogues.
                       Other: to develop the children's creativity in English.

DESCRIPTION   The children write an episode for a superhero story of their own. They invent the characters and then create a storyboard to which they add dialogue.

MATERIALS   Old magazines that can be cut up.

IN CLASS   1   Ask the children who are the typical characters in a series like 'Superman', or any of the other well-known superhero series (the good characters, the bad characters, the person with a problem, the funny characters, and so on). Tell them that they are going to invent their own superheroes.

2   Divide the children into groups of three or four and ask them to find pictures in the magazines to represent the characters. They should make a poster and give the characters names.

3   Ask them to invent a short description of their character.

4   Ask the children what usually happens in these stories; for example, someone has a problem because of the bad characters and the good characters solve the problem after a series of difficulties.

5 Ask the children in each group to invent a story using the characters and to represent it in a flow chart like the one in 5.24, 'Starlet', Worksheet 5.24 (b)3.

6 Ask the children to work in pairs and write the dialogue for each box in the flow chart.

7 When the pairs have finished, tell them to make the play script by putting the dialogues in order. You will probably need to help at the stage to ensure that the play is coherent. The children cast the play and rehearse it as described in Chapter 6.

COMMENTS

You can do this activity as a whole class up to step 5, at which point the children work on the dialogue in groups.

VARIATION 1

Use another genre with which the children may be familiar; for example fairy stories, Rudyard Kipling's *Just So Stories*, legends, and so on.

VARIATION 2

Use the same technique to dramatize a story that the children have read.

6 Role plays and improvisation

In role plays and improvisations the children are asked to assume a role and act out a situation, using whatever language they have. The roles may be characters that the children recognize from their everyday lives (doctor and patient, parent and child, bus driver and passenger), or fantasy characters (princess and dragon, space visitors to Earth, animals in a zoo). Role play is usually more successful if it involves problem solving, for example, 6.6, 'Just imagine', or if there is a task to be carried out as in 6.1, 'The market', rather than simply acting out a situation until it runs out of momentum. At higher levels, role play can be used to explore situations which the children will come across in real life: the resolution of dilemmas, assigning tasks, sharing resources, making and keeping rules, and so on. This kind of 'educational' role play allows children to explore issues in a non-threatening way and can lead to interesting discussions. I have only included a few examples as the children need quite a high language level. If you are interested in exploring the idea further, see *Drama* in the Scholastic Bright Ideas series, which have inspired many of the activities in this chapter.

A role play can be quite simple, requiring little preparation and few props, or more elaborate, requiring you to spend time preparing the language and setting up the situation (as in 6.1, 'The market'). Role plays may involve two or three children, or the whole class.

There are usually three stages to doing a role play or improvisation in class. In the first stage, the teacher prepares the children for the role play by setting up the situation and making sure the children have the necessary language. In the second, the children do the role play and the teacher observes them, noting down comments in preparation for stage three. At this point, it is important not to interfere unless absolutely necessary. Once the role play is finished, the teacher organizes reflection and feedback on the process (how the children did the activity) and the product (how it turned out).

In practice, the basic steps in preparing a role play could be:

– introduce or elicit and practise the language the children need;
– introduce the characters: here you might give the children a role card with the information they need to play their role;
– introduce the situation and present the children with the task;
– practise some typical dialogues in a more controlled environment;

– do the role play;
– feedback from the teacher and children: how did the children do the task and how well did they complete it?

These steps are given as a guide. You can of course change and adapt them as you wish.

Most of the role plays in this chapter are designed for use with the whole class working together. The classroom is the setting for a scenario and each child takes a role: they tend to become deeply involved in the action and there is generally a good atmosphere. Mixed-ability classes respond well too, as each child can use the language they are comfortable with: those with a greater language resource are able to hold more elaborate conversations, while those who feel less confident can stay with the basic dialogue. Some are suitable for children with a limited knowledge of English, and there are others which will encourage children at a higher level to be creative and to use the language they know in an unpredictable situation.

There are other activities which use improvisation in the book, for example, 4.5, 'Animating the textbook', and 1.4, 'Find your partner'; 4.6, 'From situation to dialogue'.

6.1   The market

LEVEL	1, 2
AGE GROUP	B, C
TIME	**4 × 50 minutes**
AIMS	**Language:** to practise shopping language, fruit and vegetable vocabulary, numbers. **Other:** improvisation, taking on a role.
DESCRIPTION	After some language work, the classroom is set up as a market place. The children are either shoppers, with the task of buying a number of things as cheaply as possible, or stallholders whose task is to make as much money as possible.
MATERIALS	Fruit and vegetables, either real or pictures, 'money' (counters or cut-out copies of real money), blank price tags for the fruit and vegetables, tables, aprons and shopping bags, blu-tack; feedback questionnaires like the ones in 5.1, 'Telling the story with puppets'.
PREPARATION	1 Decide which fruit and vegetables there will be in the market. If you are going to use fresh fruit, decide on four or five cheap fruits and vegetables: for example carrots, potatoes, apples, oranges, and lemons. If you are using pictures then the range can be much wider.

2 If you don't have the real thing, find pictures of fruit and vegetables.

3 Make price tags.

4 Make feedback questionnaires like the ones in 5.1, 'Telling the story with puppets'.

IN CLASS

Presenting or revising fruit and vegetable vocabulary (lesson one)

Use the pictures to teach the names of the fruit and vegetables. Here is one suggestion if you have room:

1 The children and teacher stand in a circle. Show the children the flashcards, say the word, and then put the card in the middle of the circle.

2 Say the words and get the children to point to the appropriate flashcard in the middle.

3 Repeat the words and encourage the children to say the words with you.

4 Pick up the flashcards. Cross the circle and hand a card to a child, saying the word clearly. That child should then cross the circle, hand the card to another child, and say the word clearly, and so on. Hand the rest of the cards to different children until you have none left and the children are criss-crossing the circle, handing over the flashcards and saying the word.

5 Tell everyone to sit down. Write the words on the board for the children to copy.

6 Teach *Can I have a cabbage/a kilo of bananas, please? Here you are.* The children practise by asking you, and each other, for the flashcards.

7 Ask the children to draw pictures of the fruit and vegetables. You can use these in the next lesson on the market stall.

8 Tell the children to make copies of coins: place one under a piece of paper and rub over it with a pencil until the image appears. Cut it out. (You could simply photocopy the coins for the children to cut out.)

Practising asking about prices and building a dialogue (lesson two)

IN CLASS

1 Show the children coins in your currency and tell them how to name and pronounce them in English (for example, *euro, pesetas, dollars, yen, francs, lire, baht,* or *drachma*).

2 Hold up combinations of coins and ask *How much?* Elicit the answer from learners. Get the children to do the same to each other in pairs.

3 Draw a market stall on the board, fill it with the fruit and vegetable flashcards and any pictures the children have drawn.

4 Ask the children *How much is a kilo of bananas?* and write their answer on a price tag.

5 Use the stall to practise the question and answer. (*How much is a kilo of bananas? 200 drachmas.*)

6 Teach the children *That's very expensive* and an answer like: *OK then, 150 drachmas.*

7 Set the situation with the children: a man wants to buy a kilo of apples, he goes to the market. Draw the man and stallholder on the board, leaving room to write the dialogue between them. Ask the children to suggest what the dialogue might be and write it up on the board. A basic dialogue may be something like this, though children with more language will probably suggest other alternatives.

EXAMPLE

> A Good morning.
> B Good morning.
> A How much is a kilo of apples?
> B 200 drachmas.
> A That's very expensive.
> B OK then. 150 drachmas.
> A OK. Can I have a kilo please?
> B Here you are. 150 drachmas please.
> A Here you are. Thank you. Goodbye.
> B Goodbye.

8 Practise the dialogue in chorus and then in pairs. Then substitute key words with pictures and practise it again.

9 Ask the children for other useful phrases, add them to the dialogue, and practise it again. This is especially important if you are using the role play with children who have more English. Make it clear to them that they can use any language in the role play.

FOLLOW-UP

The children write the dialogue (or variations on it) in their notebooks.

Preparing the role play (lesson three)

IN CLASS

1 Explain that in the next lesson the classroom is going to become the market place and that some of the children will be stallholders and others shoppers.

2 Explain that the stallholders will set up their stalls. Then the shoppers must buy a kilo each of five different products. (One piece of fruit represents one kilo.) Shoppers and stallholders can bargain over the price. The shoppers should try to spend as little money as possible, and the stallholders should try to make as much money as possible. Tell the children that you are going to be a language policeman and will fine anyone who does not speak in English!

3 Ask the children which role they want to take. A good ratio of shoppers to stallholders is two shoppers to one stallholder. Then tell each group what they need to bring or what you will supply.

Shoppers: some fruit and vegetables, or pictures of fruit and vegetables (if this is not possible you can use coloured bricks or pieces of card to represent the fruit); money, either cut-out coin rubbings or photocopies. A bag to put the shopping in.

Stallholders: some fruit and vegetables; money, either cut-out coin rubbings or photocopies; a piece of paper with the prices of the fruit and vegetables written on it; stallholders can also wear an apron and prepare a name board for their stall.

4 For children with more language, make feedback questionnaires like the ones in 5.1, 'Telling the story with puppets'.

Doing the role play (lesson four)

1 If you can, set up the classroom before the children come in. You need to clear away all the tables and chairs, leaving a table for each stallholder.

2 Let the stallholders in first to set up their stalls. While they are doing this, go over the shoppers' instructions with them. When the stall are set up, go over the instructions with the stallholders.

3 When everything is ready, and with a final reminder about speaking English and the 'language policeman', declare the market open and let the shoppers in.

4 When the shoppers finish buying, send them to one side to count their money and work out how much they have spent.

5 When everyone has finished, tell the stallholders to work how much money they have made.

6 Find out who has spent the least and made the most money.

7 Put the furniture back in place and do some reflection on the improvisation. You may like to give out a questionnaire, or it may be more appropriate to ask the whole class some questions about the experience. You need to find out if they enjoyed it, how much English they spoke, what they think they did well and where they could improve.

FOLLOW-UP

If you are able to take photos of the improvisation, you can make a collage to display in the school.

VARIATION

Instead of a fruit and vegetable market you can hold a jumble sale. This is a typically English event where people donate things they no longer want—toys, clothes, kitchen items, and so on—to the jumble sale. The money from the sale is given to a good cause. This idea was suggested to me by Covadonga Rodriguéz Argüelles.

6.2   Tourists

LEVEL	2, 3
AGE GROUP	**B, C**
TIME	**20 minutes to prepare the dialogue; 40 minutes to do the role play.**

AIMS

Language: to use the language of description (*There is/are*) and to activate town vocabulary (*cinema, supermarket, library, chemist, park, tourist office, museum, church, restaurant*).
Other: taking on a role, improvising with the language they have.

DESCRIPTION

The children take the roles of tourists and pedestrians. The tourists ask the pedestrians about places in the town, and the pedestrians tell them where to find them.

MATERIALS

Mini role cards for the tourists and pedestrians (see Worksheet 6.2).

PREPARATION

1 Photocopy the role cards.
2 Draw a picture of a tourist on one side of the board, with a thought bubble coming out of her head. Write or draw one of the places from a town in the bubble. On the other side of the board draw a pedestrian.

IN CLASS

1 Explain the situation to the children. The tourist wants to find the place in the bubble.
2 Build up a simple dialogue on the board with the children.

EXAMPLE

> A Excuse me?
> B Yes?
> A Is there a pizzeria near here?
> B Yes, over there/No, I'm sorry, there isn't.
> A Thank you. Goodbye.
> B Goodbye.

3 Help the children learn the dialogue by rubbing out words and either leaving them blank, or replacing them with a picture. Each time you rub out some words the children repeat the dialogue in pairs, until they know it.

If you are using this role play with children with more language facility, you can ask them for alternatives to each line. Make it clear to them that they can use any of the alternatives when they are doing the role play.

4 Give out the role play cards. The cards of the tourists have three cards, each with a thought bubble with a place they want to go to in it. The pedestrians have a map with three places in the town marked on it.

5 Ask the children to mingle and talk together. When a tourist finds a pedestrian who can tell them where the place they are looking for is, they should give the appropriate card to the teacher. When they have 'found' all three places they should sit down.

6 When most of the tourists are sitting down, stop the activity. Ask the children to reflect on the process. You can ask them how much English they used, and if they would like to know some other words and phrases before repeating the activity. Give them your opinion of their work, emphasizing what they did well and suggesting ways of improving.

7 Repeat the activity, the children changing roles.

VARIATION

You can make a model town with the children and use it to prepare the role cards.

6.3   At a restaurant

LEVEL

2, 3

AGE GROUP

B, C

TIME

30 minutes to prepare for the role play; 30 minutes to do it.

AIMS

Language: to activate the vocabulary of food, and practise asking and ordering.
Other: taking on a role, improvising.

DESCRIPTION

In this role play, the children take the parts of customers, waiters and waitresses, and cooks. They each have a role card which gives them specific information about their character and they add some extra information to personalize it. The aim of the customers is to get the meal they want, the waitresses and cooks aim to get tips by giving good service. All the children prepare the menu and the food and then the role play starts.

MATERIALS

Colours and paper to make the food; paper plates or circles of card; plastic or photocopied money; aprons for the waiters/waitresses and hats for the cooks; Worksheets 6.3 (a) and (b).

IN CLASS

Preparing for the role play

1 Tell the children that you are going to turn the classroom into a restaurant. Ask them what characters you will need (customers, waiters/waitresses, and cooks).

2 Write 'Starters', 'Main courses', 'Desserts', and 'Drinks' on a section of the board. Ask for suggestions for each category. Give each dish a price.

3 Divide the children into small groups. Ask each group to draw quick pictures of the food on the menu. It is important that there are at least two pictures of each dish. They will use these pictures in the role play. They can do the pictures at home.

Doing the role play

4 Divide the board into three columns, headed 'Customers', 'Waiters and waitresses', and 'Cooks'. Ask the children who would say *We'd like a table for three, Are you ready to order?*, and *There aren't any hamburgers left*. Ask them for more suggestions for each column. Alternatively, you may like to copy Worksheet 6.3 (b) and ask them to mark who says what.

5 Explain how the role play works: the customers have to order a meal from the menu. The waiters/waitresses have to take the order and ask the cooks for the food. The cooks have to give the waiters/waitresses the food if they have it on their cards. If not, the waiters have to ask another cook. The customers give the waiters a tip at the end of the meal if they are satisfied with the service and the food.

6 Divide the class into 'Customers', 'Waiters and waitresses', and 'Cooks'. Give each child a role card, see Worksheet 6.3 (a). Give them time to read their cards. Check that they understand what they have to do by getting them to tell you.

7 Arrange the class as a restaurant if you can. You need a dining area and a kitchen. Tell the cooks to go to the kitchen, the customers to wait at the door, and the waiters and waitresses to stand near the tables. Give each cook some paper plates and the pictures of the dishes that the children have prepared: not all the cooks will have all the dishes. Give the waiters the menus and the customers the money.

8 Start the role play by acting as the head waiter and showing the customers to their tables. When most of the customers have paid their bills, stop the role play.

9 Find out which waiter received the most tips. Ask the children to reflect on their work and to tell you what they did well and where they could improve.

FOLLOW-UP

Repeat the role play another day with the children in different roles.

6.4 First lines

LEVEL	3
AGE GROUP	C
TIME	**20 minutes**

AIMS

Language: to encourage oral fluency and encourage the use of the children's whole language resource.
Other: to stimulate creativity.

DESCRIPTION

The children invent a conversation starting with the first line the teacher gives them. The conversation should tell a story. They show their conversation to the rest of the class.

PREPARATION

Think of a first line that fits in with the topic or theme you are working on. See box for examples.

EXAMPLES

> Why are you so dirty?
> I think we're lost.
> Why are you late?
> Oh no, I've forgotten the picnic!

IN CLASS

1 Explain the activity to the class. You are going to give them a first line and they must develop a conversation from it. Give them an example first line. Ask them who they think said it and who that person was talking to. Accept all the children's suggestions and then select two characters and develop the conversation as a class.

2 Divide the children into pairs, or groups of three. Check that they know what they have to do and then write a new first line on the board. Remind them that they must decide who the characters are in their dialogue. Give them a time limit, and let them start working.

3 As the children are working, go around the class helping where necessary.

  When most of the children have finished, stop the activity. Ask for some volunteers to show their conversation.

4 Children and teacher give feedback on the process and the product.

VARIATION

You can give the children last lines instead of first lines.

6.5   Become someone different

LEVEL	3
AGE GROUP	C
TIME	**15 minutes to create the characters, 15 minutes to do the role play.**
AIMS	**Language:** to develop oral fluency and listen for detail. **Other:** to assume a role using a prop and to encourage creativity and quick thinking.
DESCRIPTION	The children work in groups of five or six. Each child takes a prop and develops a character from it. The teacher gives the children a situation and they develop a conversation in character.
MATERIALS	A selection of props, such as different hats, bags, umbrellas, newspapers, scarves, and head scarves. A role card for each child (see personal file card in 4.8 'Puppet conversations').
PREPARATION	Find the necessary props and decide on the setting for the improvisation. Possible settings are: in a dark street, hunting for a criminal, in a zoo full of escaped animals, at a football match, at a party.

IN CLASS

1 Draw a role card, like the personal file card in 4.8, page 000, on the board (include things like 'hobbies', 'age' and 'family'). Show the children one of the props. Ask them to imagine the person it belongs to and help you complete the role card on the board.

2 Give each child, or pair of children, a prop. Ask them to imagine the person the prop belongs to, and complete a role card in their books for that person.

3 Divide the class into groups of five or six. If the children have prepared the role cards in pairs, the groups should be of 10 or 12. The children in the pair take it in turns to play their part in the role play.

4 Explain the situation: they are in a zoo full of escaped animals and they should develop a conversation while they are hiding behind the elephant enclosure. Ask the children for some conversation starters.

> The zookeeper shouldn't have opened the doors!
> Is that an elephant I can see over there?
> Look out for the tiger!

Then get the groups started. You may need to help them to get going, but resist the temptation to interfere if possible.

5 Stop the improvisation when it seems to be slowing down. Comment on the children's work and ask for their comments too. Then get the other child in each pair to do the role play. You can use the same situation or change it.

FOLLOW-UP

When both groups have finished, you may like to do some language work, writing up incorrect sentences you have heard and asking the children to correct them. Remember that the aim of this activity is to encourage fluency. If the children feel they are being evaluated on their language, they will be more inhibited next time you do it.

6.6 Just imagine

LEVEL

3

AGE GROUP

C

TIME

25 minutes

AIMS

Language: to use functional language and encourage oral fluency.
Other: to explore ways of solving problems.

DESCRIPTION

The children work in groups of four or five. The teacher describes a situation in which there is conflict, or a problem to solve. The children act out their reactions to the situation.

PREPARATION

Prepare the situation; there are some examples in the box.

IN CLASS

1 Choose the situation and set the scene. If you feel the children need some support, ask the class what they could do in that situation. Write the suggestions on the board.

2 Divide the children into groups of three or four. Explain that they are in the situation and have to decide what to do. Go from group to group, starting the activity by summarizing the situation as if you were one of the children, for example, in situation 1: *The ball is over there, on the road, and breaktime is going to finish in five minutes. What can we do?*

EXAMPLES

Situation 1

The children are playing football and the ball goes over the wall and on to the main road. The school rules say that children must not go outside the gate. The teacher on playground duty is not in the playground as she is looking after a little boy who has cut his knee badly.

Situation 2

The children come out of a shop. One of the children finds some sweets from the shop in her pocket. She can't remember taking them. What should they do?

Situation 2

The children come out of a shop. One of the children finds some sweets from the shop in her pocket. She can't remember taking them. What should they do?

Situation 3

Two children start to argue about a pen. They each say it is theirs. What do the other children do? What does the teacher do?

Situation 4

It is lunchtime. The children don't like the food. What do they do? What do their parents say?

3 While the children are working, go around the class listening, and perhaps noting down words and phrases that the children need, but haven't got. You may also like to note down important language errors on which you need to do some more work in later classes.

4 Stop the activity after 5–10 minutes and ask each group if they have reached a solution. Discuss the various solutions with the class.

5 Ask the children if there were things they wanted to say, but couldn't. Supply the correct language and also any other words and phrases you noted down in step 3.

FOLLOW-UP

Repeat the activity in different groups in this or another lesson.

6.7 The quiz show

LEVEL

3

AGE GROUP

C

TIME

50 minutes to prepare the show, 50 minutes to do the improvisation.

AIMS

Language: to encourage oral fluency and to practise question forms.
Other: to encourage spontaneity and practise taking on a role.

DESCRIPTION

The children prepare and act out a quiz show. In the first lesson they prepare the questions and distribute the roles. In the second lesson they do the improvisation. You can video the improvisation if you have the facilities.

MATERIALS

Video camera (optional).

IN CLASS

Preparing the show

1 Ask the children if they watch quiz shows. Which are their favourites? Why do they like them? Who takes part in a quiz show? (The quiz master, the contestants, the assistants, the audience.)

2 Tell the children that they are going to act out a general knowledge quiz show. Ask them what categories of questions there could be, and write the categories on the board. ('Sport', 'History', 'Geography', 'Music', 'Cinema', 'Literature', and so on). Divide the class into as many groups as there are categories, and ask each group to invent ten questions for their category.

3 Ask what kind of things the quiz master, assistants, contestants, and audience say and do. Make a list of useful expressions on the board. Make a basic running order which the children will follow in the next lesson. Here is one suggestion:
 — the assistants show the audience to their seats;
 — the assistants look after the contestants;
 — the quiz master welcomes the audience;
 — the assistants introduce the contestants;
 — the quiz master asks the contestants which category they want to start with.

4 Make a poster of this and put it on the wall. The children can refer to it in the next lesson.

Doing the improvisation

5 Assign the children roles (see introduction to Chapter 5). Give them time to think about their role and what they have to do and say.

6 Use the poster to remind them of the running order.

7 Set up the classroom with tables at the front for the contestants. Get the assistants to show the audience to their seats and to look after the contestants.

8 Start the show and note down any comments as they do it.

9 When the show comes to a natural conclusion, stop the improvisation.

10 Ask the children if they have enjoyed doing the activity. Would they like to repeat it another day? Do they want to change roles? What did they learn from this first experience? Be very positive in your feedback as this is a difficult activity.

FOLLOW-UP

Repeat the activity, with the children taking different roles.

6.8 Shipwreck

LEVEL	3
AGE GROUP	C
TIME	**Part 1, 30 minutes and part 2, 30 minutes.**
AIMS	**Language:** to encourage oral fluency and practise the language of discussion and suggestions. **Other:** to encourage children to think about how society works.
DESCRIPTION	In part 1, the children are shipwrecked on a desert island. They have to decide what they need to do to survive, and how to distribute the tasks on the island. In part 2, some of the children do not want to do as they are told. The children have to decide if they need rules on the island, how to make them and how to apply them.
MATERIALS	A recording of storm music, for example: Beethoven's *Sixth Symphony*, First Movement.
IN CLASS	**Arriving on the island**

Arriving on the island

1 Clear a space in the classroom. Tell the children to stand in the space. Tell them it is the sea and they are shipwrecked. If possible, play some storm music like the symphony above. As it plays, say:

The waves are big; you are trying to swim; you see an island; then you manage to get to the island.

Finish this first part with all the children sitting exhausted on the beach on the island.

2 Explain that there are no adults in the group. The children have to look after themselves. What do they need to do? Ask them to make a list of the things to do and to organize themselves into groups. Each group is responsible for one job: for example, finding food, cooking food, making shelter, and exploring the island. Each group should make a list of what they need to do. Then they should make a timetable of the things they need to do every day, and every week, and decide who is going to do what.

3 Stop the activity when each group has its list. The groups explain their list to the others in turn.

4 When all the groups have explained their ideas, talk with the whole class about how they decided to share out the work. Did boys and girls get stereotyped jobs? Did they think about who was good at doing certain things?

Making rules

5 Divide the children into groups of five or six. There should be a mixture of children from the different groups. If you are doing part 2 in a different lesson from part 1, remind the children of the jobs they assigned themselves in part 1.

6 Call one child from each group and tell them that they are going to refuse to do their jobs. They should say that they don't think anyone should tell them what to do.

7 Send these children back to their groups. They tell the other children that they are not going to do their jobs. Wait a short time for the other children to react and then stop the activity and tell them they need to decide what to do about this situation. Ask the children to think about the following points:

Do you need rules on the desert island?
How can you make the rules?
What happens if someone breaks the rules?

8 If the children decide to make rules, get them to write them out carefully and then compare them with the other groups' ideas.

9 When they have finished, ask them if they have learned anything about rules, making them and keeping them. You will probably have to do this discussion in their first language as the children will find it difficult to express their ideas in their limited English.

COMMENTS

In *Drama* (Bright Ideas series, Scholastic), this activity is carried much further. It is used to explore other issues such as using leisure time, sharing food, bargaining, deciding on leaders, and so on.

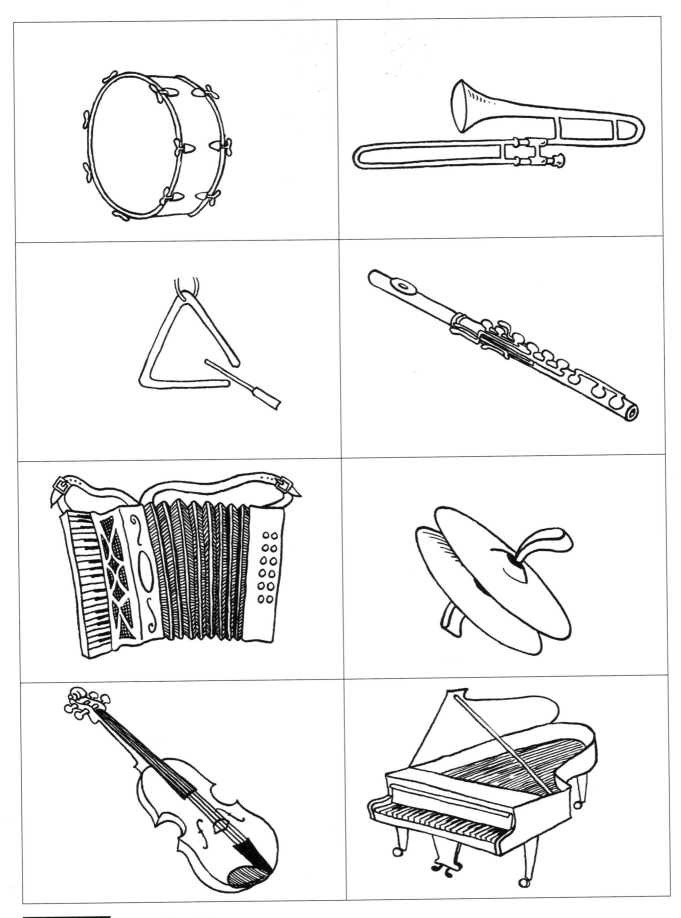

stick strips of card on for whiskers

stick on a pipe cleaner or 'twist and tie' for the tail

pipe cleaner for tail

fix a stick on the back with sticky tape

strips of card for whiskers

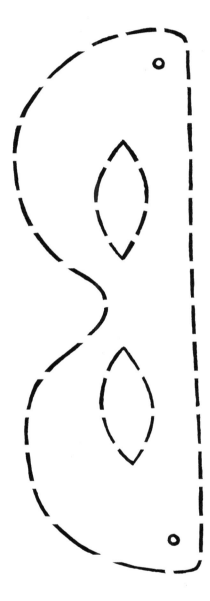

MARTY THE MARTIAN

Characters

Marty the Martian
Anna
Peter
Chris
Mrs Brown (Mrs B)
Baby Brown (Baby B)

SCENE 1

The kitchen

Anna is in the kitchen. She is eating a Mars Bar. Suddenly Marty arrives.

Anna   Oh! Who are you?

Marty   I'm Marty.

Anna   Ah. I'm Anna. And where are you from?

Marty   I'm from Mars … and … I'm hungry!

Anna   Do you like chocolate?

Marty   I love chocolate!

Anna   Here you are. Try this!

Marty   (*Eats all the Mars Bar very fast*) Ugh! I don't like chocolate!

Anna   Oh no! My Mars Bar. My Mars Bar!

Marty   I'm hungry!

Anna   Well. Let's go to Peter's.

SCENE 2

Peter's house

Peter is eating an ice cream.

Peter   Hello Anna. (*Looks at Marty*) Who are you?

Marty   I'm Marty.

Peter   Oh. Hello Marty. I'm Peter.

Marty   I'm hungry!

Peter   Do you like ice cream?

Marty   I love ice cream!

Peter   Here you are. Try this!

Marty   (*Eats all the ice cream very fast*) Ugh! I don't like ice cream!

Peter   Oh no. My ice cream. My ice cream!

Marty   I'm hungry!

Peter   Well. Let's go to Chris's.

SCENE 3

Chris's house

Chris is eating some biscuits.

Chris   Hello Peter. Hello Anna. Who are you?

Marty   I'm Marty.

Chris   Oh. Hello Marty. I'm Chris.

Marty   I'm hungry!

Chris   Do you like biscuits?

Marty   I love biscuits!

Chris   Here you are. Try this!

Marty   (*Eats all the biscuits very fast*) Ugh! I don't like biscuits!

Chris   Oh no. My biscuits. My biscuits!

Marty   I'm hungry!

Chris / **Peter** / **Anna**   } Well. Let's go to Mrs Brown's.

SCENE 4

Mrs Brown's house

Mrs Brown is giving Baby Brown his cauliflower. He doesn't like it. The others watch.

Mrs B   Here you are, lovely cauliflower.

Baby B   No, no, no. I don't like cauliflower.

Mrs B   Come on. It's nice.

Baby B   No, no, no. I don't like cauliflower.

Marty   I'm hungry!

Baby B (*Gives Marty the cauliflower*) Here you are!

Marty (*Eats all the cauliflower very fast*) Mmmm. Lovely. Delicious. I love cauliflower.

Peter
Anna } Oh, no! Ugh! Disgusting!
Chris

Mrs B Oh no! The cauliflower. The cauliflower.

Baby B Ha ha ha. My cauliflower, my cauliflower.

Marty I like cauliflower.

Peter
Anna } Oh yuck, he likes cauliflower!
Chris

CHICKEN LITTLE

Characters
Narrator
Chicken Little
Ducky Wucky
Rabbit Fabbit
Piggy Wiggy
Foxy Loxy
Chorus

SCENE 1

Narrator Once upon a time there was a chicken. Her name was Chicken Little. She lived in a little house in the country. There was a big apple tree in her garden. One day she was sitting in the garden, enjoying the sun, when suddenly an apple dropped off the tree and on to her head. She jumped up …

Chicken Little Oh no!
The sky is falling in
The sky is falling in
I must tell the king
The sky is falling in.

Narrator And off she went to tell the King.

Chorus Run Chicken, run Chicken
Run Chicken Little, run.

Narrator She went up the hill, and down the hill …

Chorus Run Chicken, run
The sky is falling in.

Narrator She went over the bridge and through the tunnel …

Chorus Chicken Little, run run
Chicken Little run run.

Narrator She went into the woods and out of the woods …

Chorus You must tell the King.
The sky is falling in!

Narrator She went round the corner … and there she met her friend Ducky Wucky.

SCENE 2

Chicken Little Hello Ducky Wucky.

Ducky Wucky Hi Chicken Little. What's the matter? Where are you going?

Chicken Little To the castle.

Ducky Wucky To the castle. But why?

Chicken Little The sky is falling in!

Ducky Wucky Oh no! The sky is falling in.

Chicken Little Yes, we must tell the King.

Together We must tell the King
We must tell the King
The sky is falling in
We must tell the King.

Ducky Wucky Come on. Let's go!

Narrator And off they went to tell the King. They went up the hill, and down the hill …

Chorus Run Chicken, run Chicken
Run Chicken Little, run.

Narrator They went over the bridge and through the tunnel …

Chorus Run Chicken, run
The sky is falling in.

Narrator They went into the woods and out of the woods …

Chorus Chicken Little, run run
Chicken Little, run run.

Narrator They went round the corner …

Chorus You must tell the king
The sky is falling in!

Narrator And there they met their friend Rabbit Fabbit.

SCENE 3

Repeat Scene 2 with Rabbit Fabbit. Change the last line.

Narrator They went round the corner and there they met their friend Piggy Wiggy.

SCENE 4

Repeat Scene 2 with Piggy Wiggy. Change the last line.

Narrator They went round the corner and there they met their friend Foxy Loxy.

SCENE 5

Chicken Little Hello, Foxy Loxy.

Foxy Loxy Hi Chicken Little. What's the matter? Where are you going?

Chicken Little To the castle.

Foxy Loxy To the castle. But why?

Chicken Little The sky is falling in!

Foxy Loxy Oh no! The sky is falling in.

Chicken Little Yes, we must tell the King.

Altogether We must tell the King
We must tell the king
The sky is falling in
We must tell the king.

Foxy Loxy Come on, follow me!

Narrator And off they went to tell the King.
They went up the hill, and down the hill …

Chorus Run Chicken, run Chicken
Run Chicken Little, run.

Narrator They went over the bridge and through the tunnel …

Chorus Run Chicken, run
The sky is falling in.

Narrator They went into the woods and out of the woods …

Chorus Chicken Little, run run
Chicken Little, run run.

Narrator They went round the corner …

Chorus You must tell the King
The sky is falling in!

All the characters go off stage.

Narrator and …

Foxy Loxy comes back on stage licking his lips and rubbing his tummy.

Narrator … nobody ever saw Chicken Little and her friends again.

CINDERELLA

Characters
Cinderella A
Cinderella B
Stepmother
Stepsister 1
Stepsister 2
Rat 1
Rat 2
Fairy Godmother
Prince

SCENE 1

The kitchen

Stepmother (*Shouting*) Cinderella!

Cinderella A Yes?

Stepsisters 1 and 2 (*Shouting*) Cinderella!

Cinderella A Yes?

Stepsister 1 Come here!

Stepsister 2 Come here!

Stepmother Wash my dress!

Cinderella A OK.

Stepsisters 1 Clean my shoes!

Cinderella A OK.

Stepsister 2 Clean my boots!

Cinderella A OK.

Stepmother Hurry up now! Go away!

Stepsisters 1 Cinderella!

Cinderella A Yes?

Stepsister 1 Go away!

Stepsister 2 Go away!

Stepmother Go away!

SCENE 2

The kitchen

Stepsister 1 Look!

Stepsister 2 What?

Stepmother What?

Stepsister 1 A letter!

Stepsister 2 A letter!

Stepmother (*Takes the letter and opens it*) An invitation!

Stepsister 1 Who from?

Stepsister 2 Who from?

Stepmother The Prince!

Stepsister 1 The Prince!

Stepsister 2 The Prince!

Stepmother To a party!

Stepsister 1 A party!

Stepsister 2 A party!

Stepmother Tomorrow!

Stepsister 1 Tomorrow!

Stepsister 2 Tomorrow!

All Cinderella!

SCENE 3

The kitchen

Stepmother Come on!

Stepsister 1 Hurry up!

Stepsister 2 Where's Cinderella?

Stepmother Cinderella!

Stepsisters 1 and 2 Cinderella!

Cinderella A Yes?

Stepmother Where's my dress?

Stepsister 1 My shoes!

Stepsister 2 My boots!

Stepmother Cinderella! Hurry up!

Cinderella A Yes, yes, yes!

Stepmother Girls! Are you ready?

Stepsisters 1 and 2 Yes, yes.

Cinderella A Yes.

Stepmother Cinderella!

Cinderella A Yes.

Stepmother Stay here!

Cinderella A Here?

Stepmother In the kitchen!

Cinderella A In the kitchen?

Stepmother Yes, clean the kitchen!

Cinderella A Clean the kitchen?

Stepmother That's right.

Stepsister 1 and 2 Goodbye!

Stepmother Goodbye!

SCENE 4
The kitchen

Cinderella is crying.

Rat 1 Look, it's Cinderella.

Rat 2 She's crying.

Rat 1 and 2 Poor Cinderella.

Rat 1 What's the matter?

Cinderella A I'm tired.

Rat 1 Cheer up!

Rat 2 What's the matter?

Cinderella A I'm sad.

Rat 2 Cheer up.

Rat 1 Don't cry!

Rat 2 No, don't cry!

The Fairy Godmother appears.

Cinderella A Who are you?

Fairy Godmother Your fairy godmother!

Rat 1 Who's she?

Rat 2 Her Fairy Godmother!

Cinderella A My Fairy Godmother!

Fairy Godmother Come on. Your wishes!

Cinderella A What wishes?

Fairy Godmother } Come on! Come on!
Rats 1 and 2 } Your wishes.

Cinderella A Oh, my wishes!

Fairy Godmother Number one?

Cinderella A A dress—please.

Fairy Godmother A dress! (*Magics a dress—the lights go off and Cinderella A changes places with Cinderella B*)

Rats 1 and 2 Ooh—a dress.

Fairy Godmother Number two?

Cinderella B Shoes—please.

Fairy Godmother Shoes! (*Magics some shoes*)

Rats 1 and 2 Ooh—shoes.

Fairy Godmother Number three?

Cinderella B A car—please.

Fairy Godmother A car! (*Magics a car*)

Rats 1 and 2 Ooh—a car.

Cinderella B Thank you!

Fairy Godmother OK. Goodbye!

Cinderella B Come on Rats!

Rats 1 and 2 Goodbye, goodbye!

Fairy Godmother Wait, wait!

Cinderella B What?

Fairy Godmother Come home at 12 o'clock.

Cinderella B OK. 12 o'clock.

Rats 1 and 2 12 o'clock.

Cinderella B Goodbye!

Rats 1 and 2 Goodbye!

Fairy Godmother Goodbye!

SCENE 5

The palace

Cinderella arrives at the party.

Stepsister 1 Who's that?

Stepsister 2 I don't know.

Stepmother Who's that?

Stepsister 2 I don't know.

The Prince talks to Cinderella.

The Prince Hello!

Cinderella B Hello.

The Prince Come and dance.

Cinderella B Yes, please.

The Prince and Cinderella dance.

Stepsister 1 Look!

Stepsister 2 What?

Stepsister 1 The Prince!

Stepsister 2 What?

Stepsister 1 They're dancing!

Stepsisters 1 and 2 Oh no!

Rat 1 Look!

Rat 2 What?

Rat 1 The Prince!

Rat 2 What?

Rat 1 They're dancing!

Rats 1 and 2 Aaaah (*a romantic sigh*)

Rat 1 What's the time?

Rat 2 12 o'clock.

Rat 1 12 o'clock. Oh no!

Rat 2 Oh no, Cinderella!

Rat 1 Cinderella!

Rats 1 and 2 It's 12 o'clock!

Cinderella B 12 o'clock. Oh no!

Rats 1 and 2 Run Cinderella, run!

Cinderella B Goodbye!

Prince Goodbye?

Cinderella B Yes, it's 12 o'clock. Goodbye! (*Cinderella runs away*)

Prince Stop, stop!

Cinderella B I can't.

Prince Stop, stop!

Prince Look, a shoe!

Rat 1 A shoe!

Rat 2 Her shoe.

Prince Her shoe!

SCENE 6

Cinderella's house

The Prince has got the shoe.

Prince Is it yours?

Stepsister 1 Yes, yes!

Stepmother Yes, yes!

Prince Oh, no it isn't.

Rats 1 and 2 It isn't, it isn't.

Fairy Godmother No, it isn't.

Prince Is it yours?

Stepsister 2 Yes, yes!

Stepmother Yes, yes!

Prince Oh, no it isn't.

Rats 1 and 2 It isn't, it isn't.

Fairy Godmother No, it isn't.

Prince Is it yours?

Cinderella Yes.

Stepsisters 1 and 2 No, it isn't.

Stepmother No, it isn't.

Rats 1 and 2 Yes, it is. Yes, it is.

Fairy Godmother Yes, it is.

Prince Yes, it is.

Dance music starts.

Prince Here you are!

Cinderella Thank you.

Prince Let's dance!

Cinderella Yes, let's dance. (*Cinderella and the Prince dance together.*)

Rats Yes, yes, let's dance! (*The Rats dance together*)

Fairy Godmother Come on, let's dance! (*The Fairy Godmother and Cinderella B dance together*)

Stepsister 1 It's not fair!

Stepsister 2 It's not fair!

Stepmother It's not fair!

FIND A BIN TO PUT IT IN

Characters
Narrator
Mermaids 1, 2, and 3
Sal
Pete
Mum
Dad

Narrator Once upon a time there was a family of mermaids and mermen who lived by the beach. They swam in the sea and played on the beach.

Together What a lovely day!

Mermaid 1 The sand is white.

Mermaid 2 The water's clean.

Mermaid 3 The fishes are our friends.

Mermaid 1 The sun is bright.

Mermaid 2 The rocks are warm.

Mermaid 3 I hope it never ends.

Narrator Then a family of humans came to the beach.

Together What a lovely beach!

Sal I want to eat.

Pete I'm hungry too.

Mum Wait a minute please.

Dad Your picnic, Pete. And one for Sal.

Mum And Dad wants ham and cheese.

Narrator The mermaids and mermen saw the humans and decided to hide.

Mermaids Humans, quick hide.

Mermaid 1 Don't move, keep still.

Mermaid 2 Keep still, don't move.

Mermaid 3 Wait until they go.

Mermaid 1 Don't move, keep still.

Mermaid 2 Keep still, don't move.

Mermaid 3 And they will never know.

Narrator The mermaids watched while the humans ate their picnic.

Mermaid 1 What's that? look, look.

Mermaid 2 Look look, what's that?

Mermaid 3 Flying through the air.

Mermaid It's rubbish.

Mermaid 2 From their picnic.

Mermaid 3 Going everywhere.

Mermaid 1 A can, a bag,

Mermaid 2 A cup, a pot,

Mermaid 3 And a banana skin.

Mermaid 1 A dirty rag,

Mermaid 2 Some silver foil,

Mermaid 3 A fizzy drink tin!

Mermaid 1 What a stink!

Mermaid 2 What a mess!

Mermaid 3 What a horrid sight!

Mermaid 1 It's theirs I think.

Mermaid 2 Yes, throw it back.

Mermaid 3 Let's have a rubbish fight.

Narrator So the mermaids and mermen started throwing the rubbish back at the humans.

Mum What's that? Look, look!

Dad Look, look, what's that?

Mum Flying through the air.

Sal It's rubbish.

Pete From our picnic.

Together Going everywhere.

Mum A can, a bag,

Dad A cup, a pot,

Mum And a banana skin.

Sal A dirty rag,

Pete Some silver foil,

Together A fizzy drink tin!

Mum What a stink!

Dad What a mess!

Mum What a horrid sight!

Sal Let's find a bin,

Pete To put it in,

Together And stop this rubbish fight!

Narrator So the family of humans picked up all their rubbish and put it in the bin. And then the mermaids and the humans enjoyed the beach together.

Mermaid 1 The sand is white.

Mermaid 2 The water's clean.

Mermaid 3 The fishes are our friends.

Children The sun is bright.

Mum and Dad The rocks are warm.

All I hope it never ends.

THAT'S FUNNY

Characters
Nicky, a cleaner
Jerry, a cleaner
Detective Smart, a detective
Slow, the detective's assistant
Al, a caretaker
Pat, a caretaker
Four children

The stage area is divided into three parts: the hall, where the concert will take place, the kitchen, and Detective Smart's office. When the children are not involved in the action, they should keep still.

SCENE 1
The hall

Nicky and Jerry are preparing the hall for the concert, putting up balloons and streamers. The children creep in and take some balloons.

Detective Smart and Slow are in the office. Slow is reading the paper.

Nicky Look!

Jerry What?

Nicky They've disappeared!

Jerry What? What's disappeared?

Nicky Those balloons! Eight balloons! They've gone!

Jerry Well, that's funny! Where can they be?

Nicky I don't know. Call Detective Smart!

Jerry Detective Smart. Hello. They've gone!

Detective Smart What's gone?

Jerry Eight balloons!

Detective Smart Eight balloons. Don't worry! I'll find them.

Jerry Thank you, Detective Smart. Goodbye.

Detective Smart Goodbye! Well, well, well. Eight balloons. What a funny thing to steal.

Slow Detective Smart, look, look at this. There's a concert …

Detective Smart Be quiet! I'm thinking.

SCENE 2
Another part of the hall

Al and Pat are working. The children creep in and take some bits of wood.

Detective Smart and Slow are in the office. Slow is reading the paper.

All Look!

Pat What?

Al They've disappeared!

Pat What? What's disappeared?

Al Those blocks. Those wooden blocks. They've gone!

Pat That's funny! Where can they be?

Al Don't know. Call Detective Smart!

Pat Detective Smart. Hello. They've gone!

Detective Smart What's gone?

Al Some wooden blocks.

Detective Smart Wooden blocks! Don't worry! I'll find them.

Al Thank you, Detective Smart. Goodbye.

Detective Smart Goodbye! Well, well, well. Wooden blocks. What a funny thing to disappear.

Slow Detective Smart, look, look at this. There's a concert with big prizes …

Detective Smart Be quiet! I'm thinking.

SCENE 3
The kitchen

Nicky and Jerry are working. The children creep in and take some saucepan lids.

Detective Smart and Slow are in the office. Slow is reading the paper.

Jerry Look!

Nicky What?

Jerry They've disappeared!

Nicky What? What's disappeared?

Jerry The saucepan lids! They've gone!

Nicky That's funny! Where can they be?

Jerry I don't know. Call Detective Smart!

Nicky Detective Smart. Hello. They've gone!

Detective Smart What's gone?

Nicky Some saucepan lids.

Detective Smart Some saucepan lids. Don't worry! I'll find them.

Nicky Thank you, Detective Smart. Goodbye.

Detective Smart Goodbye! Well, well, well. Some saucepan lids. What a funny thing to disappear!

Slow Detective Smart, look, look at this. There's a concert with big prizes tonight … .

Detective Smart Be quiet! I'm thinking.

SCENE 4
The hall

Al and Pat are working. The children creep in and take some elastic bands.

Detective Smart and Slow are in the office. Slow is reading the paper.

Pat Look!

Al What?

Pat They've disappeared!

Al What? What's disappeared?

Pat The elastic bands. They've gone!

Al That's funny! Where can they be?

Pat I don't know. Call Detective Smart!

Al Detective Smart. Hello. They've gone!

Detective Smart What's gone?

Al The elastic bands.

Detective Smart Elastic bands. Don't worry! I'll find them.

Al Thank you, Detective Smart. Goodbye.

Detective Smart Goodbye! Well, well, well. What a funny thing to steal.

Slow Detective Smart, look, look at this. There's a concert tonight with big prizes. It says big prizes for …

Detective Smart Be quiet! I'm thinking.

SCENE 5
The kitchen

Nicky and Jerry are working. The children creep in and take some beans.

Detective Smart and Slow are in the office. Slow is reading the paper.

Nicky Look!

Jerry What?

Nicky They've disappeared!

Jerry What? What's disappeared?

Nicky The beans! The beans for lunch. They've gone!

Jerry That's funny! Where can they be?

Nicky I don't know. Call Detective Smart!

Jerry Detective Smart. Hello. They've gone!

Detective Smart What's gone?

Jerry The beans. The beans for lunch!

Detective Smart Beans. Don't worry! I'll find them.

Jerry Thank you, Detective Smart. Goodbye.

Detective Smart Goodbye! Well, well, well. Beans. What a funny thing to steal.

Slow Detective Smart, look, look at this. There's a concert tonight with big prizes. It says big prizes for the most original music.

Detective Smart Be quiet! I'm thinking.

Slow But Detective—the concert

Detective Smart I'm thinking!

Slow Original music!

Detective Smart Be quiet!

Slow Goodnight sir. I'm going to the concert!

SCENE 6
A bar with a small stage

On the stage are the balloons, the wooden blocks, the lids, yoghurt pots with beans in (maraccas), and a shoe box guitar. Everyone is there except Detective Smart.

Nicky Look, my balloons!

Al And my elastic bands!

Jerry And my lids!

Pat And my blocks!

Nicky And my beans!

All Now we understand! What a surprise!

The children come on and perform the rap. The audience does the actions.

The Odd Band Rap

Making music's
Lots of fun
With instruments
For everyone.

Listen to
The ballon beat
Move your hands
Move your feet.

Listen to
The yoghurt pot
Move your body
On the spot.

Listen to
The rubber bands
Stamp your feet
Clap your hands.

Listen to
The blocks of wood
Dance together
That feels good.

Listen to
The saucepan lids
We're the odd band
Now join in kids!

Making music's
Lots of fun
Instruments for
Everyone.

Slow And the winners are … The Odd Band!

All Well done! Very good!

The children give back the things.

Children Thank you. It was a suprise. Here you are.

Slow phones Detective Smart.

Detective Smart Hello!

Slow The concert …

Detective Smart Be quiet! I'm thinking!

STARLET

The floor space should be divided into 11 parts, including the introduction, see diagram. There is a film poster of an Egyptian mummy on the wall, or drawn on the blackboard. It says Stacy/Steve Star, in The Mummy.

Scene 3	Scene 4	Scene 7
Scene 2	Scene 9	Scene 8
	Scene 10	Scene 6
Scene 1	Introduction	Scene 5

Characters

Stan/Stacy Starlet
Starlet's Mum
Starlet's Dad
Bus Conductor
Starlet's Friend
Film Director
Film Star
Passer-by
Ambulance Attendant 1
Ambulance Attendant 2
Nurse
Robber

INTRODUCTION

To the audience

Starlet So, you want to be a star! Well, watch this!

SCENE 1

Mum Stacy! It's 9 o'clock.

Starlet It's what? Oh no, I'm late!

Mum Again! Get a move on! Bye!

Starlet Bye!

SCENE 2

In the car

Starlet Oh no!

Dad What's the matter?

Starlet There isn't any petrol in the car!

Dad Well, get the bus!

Starlet The bus. Good idea! Bye!

SCENE 3

On the bus

Starlet The High Street, please.

Bus Conductor 54p, please.

Starlet Here you are.

Conductor Thanks.

SCENE 4

On the bus

Starlet Well, hello! How are you?

Friend Hi Stacy! How's things?

Starlet Fine, fine. How's your Mum?

Friend She's fine. And your brother?

SCENE 5

On a film set

Film Star is dressed as a mummy in bandages.

Film Star I don't like you.

Director You don't?

Film Star I don't like the film!

Director You don't?

Film Star And I don't like this costume. I'm leaving. (*Film Star goes out*)

Director You are?

SCENE 6

On the street

Director I don't believe it. She's gone!

Robber Hands up!

Director What am I going to do?

Robber Your money or your life!

Director My star! My film!

Robber I said 'Your money or your life'!

Director Oh yes! (*He realizes what is happening, He faints*)

SCENE 7

On the bus

Starlet Oh no! That was my stop!

Friend Wait a minute. Don't jump!

Starlet jumps off the bus and lands in the same scene as the Film Director.

Starlet Ow, ow ow, my ankle, my arm, my legs!

Friend Too late!

SCENE 8

On the street

Passer-by Oh no! I'll call an ambulance.

Passer-by takes out a mobile phone and calls an ambulance.

Starlet Ow, ow, ow, my ankle, my arm, my legs.

Passer-by Oh dear. I think they're broken?

Starlet Of course they're broken. Ow, ow, ow. Call an ambulance.

Passer-by Don't worry it'll be here in a minute. (*Notices Film Director*) Oh look, another body.

Here's the ambulance. Take them away please.

Ambulance attendants take Starlet and the Director away to the hospital scene.

SCENE 9

In hospital

Nurse He's waking up!

Film Director Where am I?

Nurse In hospital.

Film Director Oh, what happened? What happened? My film. My film star! Where is she?

Nurse Oh, so that woman is a film star. Well, well, well. She's over there. Look.

Points to Starlet, who is covered in bandages like a mummy.

Film Director Perfect, she's perfect.

Nurse (*To Starlet*) Don't move

Starlet I can't!

Film Director Hello. How are you?

Starlet Terrible, it's been the worst day in my life.

Film Director Really?

Starlet Yes! Just look at me!

Film Director Oh yes. I see. Oh yes. Mmmm, would you like a job?

Starlet A job?

Film Director Yes, I'm looking for a film star, just like you!

SCENE 10

At the front

Starlet And that's how it all started.

All the other actors crowd round asking for autographs.

Match the sentences to the pictures in Starlet's story

A She meets an old friend on the bus and they talk and talk.

B A man calls an ambulance.

C She goes to her car but it doesn't work. Her father tells her to get the bus.

D Film Star is not happy with her part in the film *The Mummy*. She leaves.

E Starlet misses her stop so she jumps off the bus and breaks some bones.

F Film Director meets Starlet in hospital.

G Starlet becomes a famous film star.

H She gets on the bus.

I Starlet gets up late. Her mother tells her to hurry.

J A thief takes all Film Director's money, he faints.

K Starlet introduces the story.

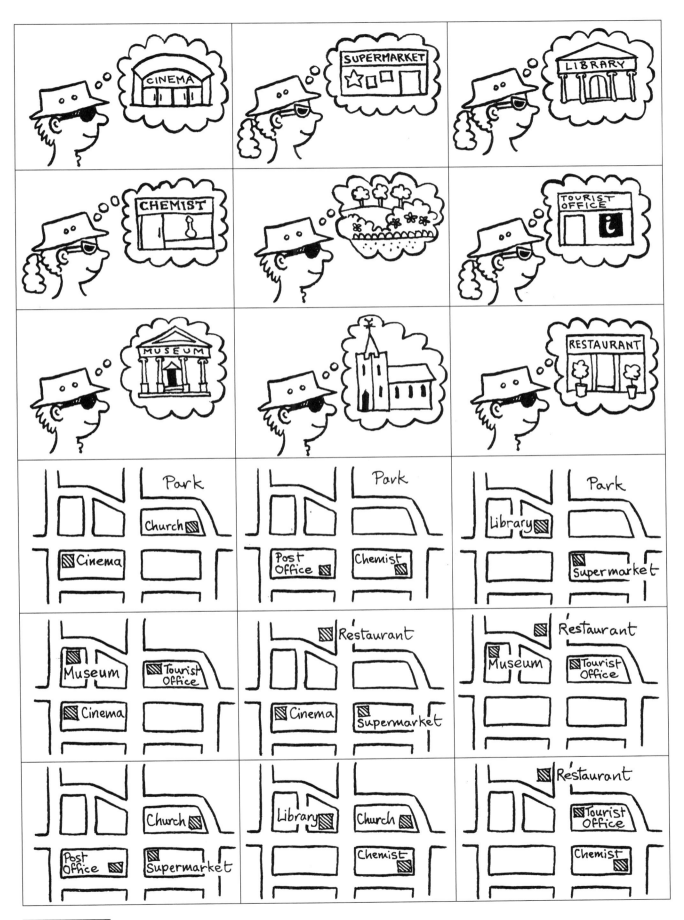

Role cards

Waiter/waitress	Cook
1 You are feeling very tired today.	**1** You are feeling very tired today.
2 You have a cold and a headache.	**2** You have a cold and a headache.
3 You want to earn a lot of tips.	**3** You don't like waiters.
4 You are in love with one of the cooks.	**4** You are in love with one of the waiters.
5 Your feet hurt.	**5** You hate your job.
6 You are in a hurry to go home.	**6** You need to make a phone call urgently.

Customer	Customer	Customer
1 You don't eat meat.	**3** You are very, very hungry.	**5** You don't like fried food.
2 You are on a diet.	**4** You don't eat eggs.	**6** You can't eat salt.

WORKSHEET 6.3(b)

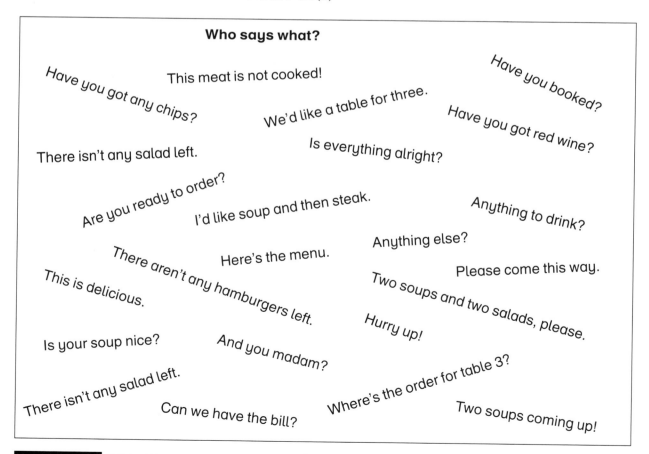

Who says what?

Have you got any chips?

This meat is not cooked!

Have you booked?

We'd like a table for three.

Have you got red wine?

There isn't any salad left.

Is everything alright?

Are you ready to order?

I'd like soup and then steak.

Anything to drink?

Here's the menu.

Anything else?

There aren't any hamburgers left.

Please come this way.

This is delicious.

Two soups and two salads, please.

Hurry up!

Is your soup nice?

And you madam?

There isn't any salad left.

Where's the order for table 3?

Can we have the bill?

Two soups coming up!

Further reading

Many stories, rhymes, chants, and poems can be adapted for dramatization, and the activities in this book are intended to suggest ways in which teachers can do this. Below are some theoretical books about using drama, as well as various fictional works which may provide useful material. This is not intended to be an exhaustive list and teachers should feel confident about selecting material of their own.

Using drama

Maley, A. and **A. Duff**. Second edition 1983. *Drama Techniques in Language Learning: A Resource Book of Communicative Activities for Language Teachers*. Cambridge: Cambridge University Press. ISBN 0 521 2886 1. A rich source of 'dramatic' ideas which can be used and adapted with young learners.

McCaslin, N. Sixth edition 1996. *Creative Drama in the Classroom and beyond*. New York: Longman. ISBN 0 801315859. How to introduce the dynamics of drama into the classroom and other settings. The text stresses the benefits of drama as a tool for helping all children develop communication and critical thinking skills. There are numerous exercises and practical suggestions for planning activities and adapting materials for use in improvisation, pantomime, movement, speech, and other dramatic arts.

Wessels, C. 1987. *Drama*. Oxford: Oxford University Press. ISBN 0 A 4370976. Resource Books for Teachers series. Gives practical ideas on using drama to promote language acquisition; to improve coursebook presentation; to teach spoken communication skills; and for revision and reinforcement.

Teaching children

Halliwell, S. 1992. *Teaching English in the Primary Classroom*. Harlow: Longman. ISBN 0 582071097. Longman Handbooks for Language Teachers series. Gives an insight into how children learn and how to achieve a positive attitude towards language learning in your classroom.

Jennings, C. 1993. *Children as Storytellers: Developing Language Skills in the Classroom*. Oxford: Oxford University Press. A practical book for classroom teachers that uses and develops children's natural talents for telling stories.

Phillips, S. 1993. *Young Learners*. Oxford: Oxford University Press. ISBN 0 19 4371956. Resource Books for Teachers series. A rich source of ideas for different activities including puppets, drama, songs, and stories.

Reilly, V. and **S. M. Ward.** 1997. *Very Young Learners*. Oxford: Oxford University Press. ISBN 0 19 437209 X. Resource Books for Teachers series. Gives advice and ideas for teaching children aged 3 to 6 years. It contains activities using songs, drama, stories, and arts and crafts.

Wright, A. 1995. *Storytelling with Children*. Oxford: Oxford University Press. ISBN 0 19 437202 20. Resource Books for Teachers series. Gives ideas for exploiting over 30 stories in class.

Wright, A. 1997. *Creating Stories with Children*. Oxford: Oxford University Press. ISBN 0 19 437204 9. Resource Books for Teachers series. Ideas for getting children to tell and write stories in English.

Songs, chants, and rhymes

Byrne, J., M. Pratt, and **A. Waugh.** 1982. *Jingle Bells*. Oxford: Oxford University Press. Book and cassette. Traditional songs for use with young learners.

Davies, L., F. Leibe, and **J. Matthews.** 1987. *Language Resources*. Bright Ideas series. Leamington Spa: Scholastic. This book has rhymes, games, dances, and poems in it. Although it is aimed at teachers of English-speaking children, some of the material can be adapted for English as a foreign language.

Cahill, N. and **M. Pratt.** 1993. *Literacy Skills Through Rhyme and Rhythm*. Oxford: Oxford University Press. A photocopiable book designed for native speaker primary teachers offering differentiated activities through rhyme and rhythm.

Graham, C. 1979. *Jazz Chants for Children*. 1988. New York: Oxford University Press. ISBN 0 19 5024974. Teacher's book, workbook, and cassette. A collection of chants which focus on English stress, rhythm, and pronunciation.

Graham, C. 1988. *Jazz Chant Fairy Tales*. New York: Oxford University Press. ISBN 0 19 4342999. Fairytales told in verse to a strong rhythm, suitable for children with several years of English.

Murphey, T. 1992. *Music and Song*. Oxford: Oxford University Press. ISBN 0 19 437055 0. Resource Books for Teachers series. Ideas for using music in the classroom. Many can be adapted and the book has a chapter on young learners.

Paul, D. 1996. *Songs and Games for Children*. Oxford: Heinemann. Songs and games grouped around target language areas.

Ward, S. 1980. *Dippitydoo*. Harlow: Longman. A book of songs with actions.

The Oxford Book of Story Poems. Oxford: Oxford University Press. An anthology of poems that tell stories.

Puppets and props

Robson, D. 1990. *Rainy Days: Puppets*. London: Franklin Watts. Lots of different kinds of puppets aimed at native speaker 7-year-olds and above. Simple instructions and colour photographs.

Wright, A. 1993 (new edition). *1000+ Pictures for Teachers to Copy*. Harlow, Essex, UK: Longman. ISBN 017 556878 2. These pictures could provide ideas for outlines of puppets.

Wizadora. Oxford: Oxford University Press. Contains several scenes which could be acted out with puppets.

Plays

Conklin, T. *Mystery Plays*. Scholastic. Detective story plays aimed at native-speaker children. Could be used with children who have a few years of English.

Oxford Playscripts. 'Owls Stages'. Oxford: Oxford University Press. Playscripts adapted from popular stories for native speaker children.

Stories

Carle, E. 1984 *The Very Hungry Caterpillar*. Harmondsworth: Penguin. A story about a baby caterpillar growing into a butterfly.

Clarke, G. 1993 *Ten Green Monsters*. London: Anderson Press. Funny story about ten monsters who fall off a wall.

Hill, E. 1999 *Where's Spot?*. London: Penguin. This practises simple structures. It is a story about a popular dog.

Rosen, M. and **H. Oxenbury.** 1989 *We're going on a Bear Hunt*. London: Walker Books. ISBN 07445 23230. An illustrated version of a well-known rhyme.

Ross, T. 1995 *Stone Soup*. London: Picture Lions, HarperCollins Publishers Ltd. A story about a clever hen who persuades a hungry wolf to taste her stone soup.

Tolstoy, A. and **H. Oxenbury.** *The Great Big Enormous Turnip*. Oxford: Heinemann. The famous story of a big turnip that is very difficult to get out of the ground.

Vipont, E. 1971 *The Elephant and the Bad Baby*. London: Puffin Books, Penguin. This is the story of a journey taken by an ungrateful baby.

Role plays and improvisation

Paul Rooyackers et al. *101 Drama Games for Children: Fun and learning with Acting and Make-believe*. California: Hunter House. Non-competitive improvisational games which include: Introduction games, sensory games, story games, and games with masks and costumes.

Useful address

The English Folk Dance and Song Society has a number of useful publications written for English speaking children, but which English language teachers could easily use in their classes. Their material is especially useful if you are teaching English culture as part of your curriculum. They take orders by phone.

The English Folk Dance and Song Society
2 Cecil Sharp House
Regents Park Road
London
NW1 7AY

Tel: 44 (0)171 485 2206
Fax: 44 (0)171 284 0523

Indexes

Activities which can be adapted to practise various structures or vocabulary topics are not listed under each separate structure.

Topics

Language

Cross-curricular themes